HOW TO BE THE
BIG
PERSON
YOUR
LITTLE PERSON
NEEDS

CLAIRE BROAD

OMNE

First published by The OMNE Group in 2015

National Library of Australia Cataloguing-in-Publication entry

Creator: Broad, Claire, author.

Title: How to be the big person your little person needs / Claire Broad.

ISBN: 9780987148155 (pbk)

Notes: Includes index.

Subjects: Child rearing.
Parent and child.
Discipline of children.
Temper tantrums in children.
Sleeping customs.

Dewey Number: 649.1

Illustrated by Simon Williams
Edited by Robert Watson
Cover design by Julia Kuris
Layout by OMNE

Printed by The OMNE Group www.omne.com.au

Book is available in bookstores and via Amazon in print and as an eBook.

To all the Little People that teach us so much
about ourselves, the world and unconditional love.

Names have been changed to protect the privacy of my clients.

CONTENTS

Part III: Top Secret Techniques 89

Acknowledgements

There are many defining moments when you embark on the journey of writing a book. The first of which is when you realise that you should write one. Thanks, Glen Carlson.

The next, is when you decide to actually do it and conjure up a plan of attack. Thank you, Andrew Griffiths.

Then, you start to write and you need a much bigger team. Thank you to all of my friends, family and accountability buddies. I'd like to use the excuse that there are too many of you to list, and while there are a lot, I feel awkward about who should be at the top of the list. So you know who you are! Then, the wheels fall off the cart. Thank you Mum, Donna, Emma, Margi, Melinda, Stefan, Rosemary, and the twenty people pestering me for the final product. This book is here because of you.

Somehow, you plod on and finish writing the book. Just when you think it's over, there is a whole other world of book production to tackle. Thank you Robert for helping me say what I really wanted to say and tidying up my word vomit. Kip for my stunning illustrations, Julia for the cover, and thanks Andrew Akratos and Omne for making my Word document a real book!

Most of all though, thank you Charlie for being there for the whole ride; I couldn't have done it without you.

INTRODUCTION

Hello there!

Welcome to my book. If you are reading this, I'm going to assume you have a Little Person around, or maybe you will soon. I know that makes it hard to sit and read quietly for a long time, so I have kept the chapters short and created simple action lists throughout the book.

This book is designed to be used as an ongoing reference book. I want it to be dog-eared and written on. 'Oh my, write on a book?! Sacrilege' I hear you gasp. Well, I am not just giving you permission, I am asking you to scribble and highlight all over this one. It will make it easy for you when you pick it up in the future to find that bit you marked with a star * or drew a smiley face next to ☺. You will find that each time you read this book it will be relevant to a new set of things happening in your family.

'How to be the Big Person your Little Person needs' is designed to get you to *do stuff*. It's useless if you don't put into practice the things you read on these pages. Knowledge without action is futile. So please, use the action lists throughout this book to modify your behaviour and reform your Little Person's in the process.

That's right. You have to change, not just your Little Person.

(Did you underline that sentence? Perhaps you should!)

Before we get to that let me tell you a little bit about who I am, and why I'm writing this book. My name is Claire and I help families and their toddlers set up positive patterns of behaviour in Little People's early lives, with these patterns lasting well into their teenage years. I work one on one with families and their Little People (generally aged from 1-7) to create a happy home and change old habits into fresh, new patterns.

Coaching was a logical progression for me, and following a decade in the Childcare industry, I decided to take my experience and knowledge and create my own business where I could help families to understand each other again. Working with literally hundreds of Little People and their families over the years meant I spent many long days with Little People and their individual personalities. And yet this still hasn't deterred me from having kids of my own one day.

In this time I had the opportunity to gain great insights into which techniques work; techniques that are effective with most children and not just one or two.

Originally I ventured into the Childcare industry after finishing school because I wanted to be able to encourage Little People in their early learning processes. I loved those early years and how nurturing their Little People personalities could shape the way in which they took on the world.

I am so lucky to have spent time in this environment; to have learnt lessons, gained skills and understand the causes of much of the despair during parenthood that is triggered when raising Little People. The kids I have watched grow are now delightful Little People, and this book will show you tried and tested techniques for helping your own Little Person to be a delight too.

This book is split into three parts and is designed to be read cover to cover the first time. Following that, I have written short chapters with links to other relevant bits in the book, so you can quickly navigate to the most useful information for you. As I said, this will be an ongoing reference book for you. As your Little Person grows through many stages, there will be different things that are relevant for you in these pages.

The Three Parts

Being the best parent you can be for your Little Person is a bit like being a tree ... bear with me here. Before a seed can grow into a tree, it must have strong roots. This strong foundation will keep it grounded throughout the rough weather it will encounter in its life. Once it has a solid foundation of roots, the plant is then free to unfurl towards the sun and grow big and tall. Over time, the trunk will thicken and get strong. Only then can it bear fruit.

As a parent, you need to get in touch with your 'inner tree'. So, what do these elements represent?

Your foundational 'roots' are how you nurture yourself. It is essential *you* take the time to look after *you* and be clear on what *you* need. Grow your roots by creating patterns of behaviour that benefit you and your mental health. Only once you have done that can you really be the Big Person your Little Person needs. Don't worry, I have created a guideline of how to do this with a Little Person in tow, in the first part of this book.

Once your roots are strong, you can begin unfurling and growing your trunk. This will happen in part two. You, as a Big Person need to learn, understand and practise the Seven 'ABCs' to Parenting. These keys are simple and often overlooked. They are the make and break for parents with toddlers, (and remember that teenagers are just the same as toddlers but with attitude, sex and drugs thrown in). So, having a strong handle on these ABCs is the secret to staying calm, being in control and offering the best guidance for your Little Person. Part two is all about these seven ABCs. Practise them to strengthen your trunk. With time they will become second nature.

Many of you will have bought this book for part three; the fruit. My top secret behaviour-change techniques. If you have a Little Person keeping you up at night, eating only white things or throwing themselves on the floor in a meltdown all the time, easy tiger. I know you are chomping at the bit to get to section three, but please, check your roots and trunk first. A tree that fruits too early will have a failed crop. Starting behaviour-changing techniques before you are ready will create much bigger problems for you in the long run.

So, what kind of fruit tree are you going to be?

I'm an apple tree (like the one on the cover).

Part I: Big People

This is a book about changing Little People's Behaviour, but two of the three parts are more about changing Big People's behaviour than Little People's. I'd like to share with you why I did that.

Through my coaching work, I have realised that that most undesirable behaviour from young children is more of a result of the parents' actions, rather than a problem with the children themselves. This is often due to a lack of knowledge of what makes Little People tick (or flip). You will find that as a parent you will discover great tools (hopefully a few later in this book) and these tools will be fantastic for a while. Sooner or later though everything will fall back to how it was before and you will need to find new tricks to manage your Little People.

This happens because there is something missing. Some key ingredient has been left out. This section holds many of those ingredients. Even more can be found in part two which is all about the fundamental concepts that that Little People need to thrive. Big People must create the foundations for calm, happy toddlers. Things like consistency, follow through and boundaries cannot be created by Little People. Big People need to develop them.

That is why I have put such a focus on Big People and how they can look after themselves and their mindset in this book. Your mindset as a parent is the thing that will have the biggest impact on your growing child, so let's make sure you give yourself a head start.

1. LOOKING AFTER THEM, AND YOU TOO

Little People are intense. They suck your energy all day and keep you up at night, they won't let you eat your whole piece of toast or go to the toilet alone. (Imagine if your partner behaved like that... would you stick around?) Parenting is one of the hardest things you will ever do, and one of the few things that you really can't run away from. It is also incredibly rewarding and, if you look after yourself and your mindset, you will find joy, even when the going gets tough. This chapter is about some of the skills you can use to look after yourself, while you raise your Little Person. 'Look after myself?' I hear you scoff, 'as if I have time for that...'

According to Beyondblue: Mental Health Information Service, Post-natal depression affects nearly sixteen percent of women giving birth in Australia. Also, studies have found three out of ten men are depressed when their child is six weeks old. This may come from a lack of social and emotional support, sleep deprivation, stress and changes in relationships (especially between partners), un-met pre-natal expectations, a negative or traumatic birth experience ... The list goes on.

It is so important that if you feel like you aren't coping that you *seek help*. A great place to start is your GP. Speak to your partner, family and friends. You will be amazed how many people are feeling the same way as you and just not talking about it.

AEROPLANE OXYGEN

You know that safety briefing on the plane that hardly anyone listens to? They say something along the lines of, 'In case there is a loss in cabin pressure, yellow oxygen masks will drop from the ceiling compartment located above you. Blah, blah, blah tighten the strap, blah, blah. *Please make sure you secure your own mask before assisting others, including children.*' Let's just imagine that for a second. You're on a plane with a Little Person on your knee. You hear a bang and the oxygen masks fall down. Your first instinct is to save your baby. The reality is however, that if you don't save yourself first, there will be nobody around to save your baby. This is a powerful concept and one I believe rings true even when you aren't on a doomed plane. There are two crucial parts to caring for yourself. Looking after your body and looking after your mind.

LOOKING AFTER YOUR BODY

Looking after your body is paramount to looking after yourself. If your body is unhealthy it will greatly affect your happiness and stress levels. If you care for your body by feeding it nutritious food and getting daily exercise, it will look after you by staying healthy. Little People are the main spreaders of contagious disease. They will spend what feels like a decade with some form of runny nose, gastro, chest infection or something. Give yourself and your immune system a head start.

How to Be the Big Person Your Little Person Needs

How? Start by Doing These Three Things:

Watch what you eat

I have spent many years learning about food and researching what is 'good' and 'bad' for my body. I was totally confused and frustrated by the huge amount of conflicting information about carbs, no carbs, paleo diets, fasting, glycaemic indexes, calories, protein and veganism (cue overwhelming feelings and confusion). I have settled on a very simple way of knowing if a food is good for me or not. I look at a food and ask myself 'How much sun is inside this?' Plants (fruits and vegetables) catch the energy from the sun so they rank highly on my 'sun scale'. Next is animal products: things like red meat, poultry, fish, eggs and minimally processed dairy products. These are second tier on the 'sun scale' because the animals we eat are usually herbivores. Their bodies are made up of the plants they eat, the plants made from the sun. So animal proteins are two steps from being sunlight. Carnivorous animals are one step further away from being energy captured from the sun.

Now, following this way of thinking, how much sunlight is there in something like lemonade? Are there even lemons in lemonade? Generally, the more processed a food is, the less sunlight it will contain.

My favourite book about this topic is called *In Defence of Food* by Michael Pollan. His key message is 'Eat food. Not too much. Mostly plants'.

The second rule I live by: the 80/20 rule. Trying to do anything perfectly takes a huge amount of energy. Especially something you usually do at least three times a day! I now eat in a 'zigzag'. If eating healthily is 'zigging' I spend most of my life in a zig. But every now and then we all need a triple-choc-caramel-fudge-brownie-with-ice-cream, so every now and then, I 'zag'. I keep to the eighty percent healthy and twenty percent 'zagging' method though.

There are many books about the huge topic of food and diet. I am no expert and I am not going to tell you what you should or shouldn't be doing. These are two little things that have helped me to create a healthier lifestyle for myself, and I encourage you to find something that works for you.

Move your body

You have Little People. I get that heading to the gym every day is a thing of the past for most of you. Trips to the park probably aren't though. Be the Big Person who gets up and runs around with the Little People. They will *love* it! Make an effort to move more around the house. Dance while you iron. Scrub the floor with gusto. Go for a walk with the stroller. Little People enjoy getting out and about too. You could even use one of your screens to do some YouTube yoga or Wii Fit or whatever you think is fun. Where there is a will, there is a way.

Sleep

A humorous heading in a parenting book! I know you'd sleep for 15 hours straight if it was an option. Seriously, you do need to make getting plenty of sleep a priority though. Perhaps you might need to call on your partner to take on some of the duties. Go to bed early. Take turns getting up in the night. If you're breastfeeding, it is okay to ask your partner to do a delivery service. Take naps when your Little People do (after you pee and shower). Especially if you have a newborn. There are plenty of strategies for managing Little People's sleep later in the book and you'll be encouraged to nip sleep issues early. Don't assume your Little People will 'grow out' of things. They often don't.

LOOKING AFTER YOUR MIND

Maintain social support

Spending all day with Little People can be great fun and really rewarding. It can also be downright exhausting and leave you feeling really isolated. Every day is different. Keeping in touch with other Big People is going to play a major role in keeping you sane. So much so, there is a whole chapter about it called *Gathering your team*.

Find hobbies and take time to pamper yourself

Having some downtime and doing things just for you is something that will probably bring mixed feelings. Know that it is a distraction from stress and a great way to relieve tension. Strung out Big People can't do the best by their Little People. So even though it may feel selfish to call time out, you should know it is actually beneficial *for everyone*.

Keep your mind sharp

Do something to keep your mind sharp. Let's be honest. Conversation with Little People isn't the most stimulating pastime. Teach yourself something. Learn a new skill. Study something by correspondence. Read books. Work part-time if it suits you. Write a book. Do crossword puzzles.

Think good things, have the right attitude

Fill your mind with good things and push out the bad. Make a conscious effort to notice negative patterns of thinking and write them down. At the end of the day, look back over your limiting beliefs. Sometimes on paper they seem much less true and it's handy to know exactly what things are whizzing around in your mind. Choose a more constructive thought and post a few sticky notes around the house with reminders of this positive message. It doesn't take long to take seed and your mind will start collecting the evidence of why these new statements are true.

When you (or your Little Person) feel anxious or frightened

There is a technique I use for recurring thoughts that frighten me or make me anxious. Have you got one of those? Perhaps when you are far from home and worry you have left the stove on. I'm going to use that one to illustrate the process, but you use your own.

So when you're driving and you are quite far from your house you begin to wonder. Did you take those boiling eggs off the stove? You can't remember. You remember putting them on though. That was ... you glance at your watch. Four hours ago. Oh no. What would happen if eggs were dry boiling for four hours? You'd better get home and check. As you drive home you seem to get every red light. The pictures in your mind get more and more dramatic. The fire brigade will be there when you turn up. Half the house will be burned down. You'll have to take the kids somewhere else for their nap. And you'll have to tell your partner. You play out the conversation in your mind.

You get the picture. So my question is, when imagining this situation are you watching yourself from afar, or are you seeing the action from your own point of view? Is it close or far away? Is it in colour or black and white? Is it vivid or dull?

For me, especially in those moments of anxiety it is like I am seeing it from my own perspective. It's big and vividly colourful. So what can you do when this happens?

Take the image and put it on a movie screen in your mind. Like a big old drive-in screen. Manipulate the movie. Turn the sound off. Make it black and white. Then shrink the screen and push it far away from you. Further and further until it is so far away you can't see it.

Doing this over and over again will make the thoughts have less power. You can even teach your Little People the same trick.

Process your emotions

Your children will emulate what they watch you do. They are very intuitive and understand all of the emotional undercurrents of the Big People around them. They will look to you to learn how to manage their own stress, excitement, fear and every other emotion. If you are prone to pushing down your negative emotions (or emotions in general), try to talk about them more. This will teach your child an emotional vocabulary, give them a healthy understanding of feelings, and how to process them.

You need to be the Big Person that your Little Person can copy. If you want a strong, independent, empathic, kind and loving Little Person, you must first *be those things*. Little People are so in tune with the emotional current of those around them. They read people better than most Big People can and they can tell if you are pretending. They know. They also learn to pretend too.

So if you are feeling anxious; be anxious and talk about how you feel and what you are doing to move through that. If you tell your Little People you are 'Fine' and pretend to be okay, guess what they will do when they feel anxious? You won't break your children by being authentic.

Develop self-love/talk

I have spent many years working on the way that I speak to myself. I still struggle to love and appreciate myself much of the time, but I am working on it. Things that have helped me are meditation, positive affirmations plastered around my house, thinking of myself as a Little Person that needs to be cared for, like I care for other Little People. Would I speak to a three year old that way? Would I feed them that? Would I expect them to stay on task for three hours? So why am I doing that to myself? Another thing to recognise is that we often assume what other people are thinking and don't then question the accuracy of our assumption.

How to Be the Big Person Your Little Person Needs

My friend said to me once:

'People aren't thinking nasty things about you. That is all in your head. They are thinking about what they had for breakfast'.

Whatever people are thinking, it doesn't matter. All that matters is what you tell yourself they are thinking. So the next time your Little Person screams blue murder in public, instead of telling yourself 'Everyone must think I'm a terrible parent' choose to think something like, 'They totally know what I'm going through, they want to come and help, but don't want to be invasive and come across as judgemental. I know they are thinking supportive thoughts'. Even though they are thinking about their breakfast, you will make yourself feel better.

Action list:

- *Look after your body*
- *Eat nourishing food*
- *Move every day*
- *Get as much sleep as you can*
- *Look after your mind*
- *Maintain social support*
- *Find hobbies and pamper yourself*
- *Keep your mind sharp*
- *Think good things and have the right attitude*
- *Practise minimising your anxious thoughts*
- *Process your emotions*
- *Develop self-love/talk*

How to Be the Big Person Your Little Person Needs

2. Gathering Your Team

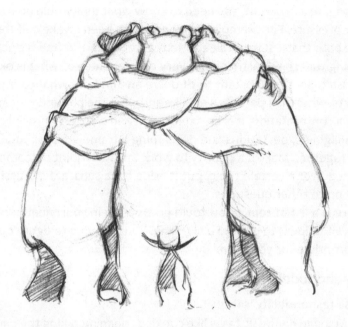

As a parent, it is really important that you surround yourself with great people that will *help* rather than hinder you.

You will find that many of the friends you had before you had children will have different interests to you now and some may fade away into the background. That is okay though, because you are about to meet some of your greatest friends!

From the day your Little Person was born you were meeting lots of new people. This is fortunate because it really does take a village to raise a child. You will probably have acquired a Mothers' Group, and met other parents, your Little Person will continue to make new friends at the park and you will end up talking to their parents. You'll befriend teachers and babysitters, maybe even a nanny will join your family. Let's look at these relationships in more detail.

YOUR PARTNER

The most important team member is your partner (assuming you have one) and I would highly recommend calling an official team meeting with him/her. Use this time to ask questions about their ideals and attitudes towards life as a parent. You need to know what they would do when put under pressure. For example: if you had both been awake half the night with a baby that just won't sleep. Many parents learn at four o'clock in the morning that their partner has a very different idea of what is okay and what isn't. So it's important to sit down and find out what your partner expects, what their parents were like and what their boundaries are. This is not a confrontation, it is an exploration and discovery process, aimed at managing expectations and developing a framework for you both to work together. Make it a priority to work towards a joint outcome. If you disagree over a certain topic, put it aside for a separate discussion and move on to other questions.

Here is a list of topics you could go through in your meeting: (This is just a list of ideas to get the ball rolling. You will need to figure out what is appropriate for your family).

Baby and toddler stage:

Whose responsibility is it to:

- Manage domestic tasks like cooking, cleaning taking the nappy bin out (ew!), etc?
- Get up and tend to the baby in the night?
- Manage the expenses of the family?
- How will you manage your income as well as raising your family? Who will work, what hours?
- What are the expectations around childcare?
- Who will be responsible for picking up the baby when the phone rings at 10am "Come and pick up little Emily because she is vomiting and has a high temperature"?
- How will you handle each other's parents? What are the boundaries around that?
- How many Little People will there be? What are your thoughts on only children?
- How will you discipline your Little Person? What for?

How to Be the Big Person Your Little Person Needs

- How long do you think a baby should be left to cry?
- What would you do if the baby wouldn't stop crying?
- How would you handle a temper tantrum?
- What about rocking to sleep? Dummies? Controlled crying? Co-sleeping? What do you feel strongly about?
- Surrounding discipline and settling, what *isn't* okay?
- How can Big People manage anger? Is it okay to yell? How can you ask for help if you need a break?

School age:

- Public or private education?
- How will your careers change?
- If you're juggling work, will you use after school care or a nanny?
- Again, who will leave work to pick up a sick child from school?
- How will you manage domestic duties, after school activities, and meals?
- Whose job is it to take the kids to soccer on the other side of the city?
- What about all the birthday parties?
- What should school lunches consist of, and who will pack them?
- How much screen time is too much?

GRANDPARENTS

Grandparents are a bit of a mixed bag. You might be blessed and have amazingly supportive parents and in-laws who actually help you, or maybe they make life a bit challenging. Whichever is true, remember that you are the Big Person and you have the right to make decisions. Your Little Person is your priority and sometimes it's necessary to go a little bit Mumzilla (or Dadzilla).

YOUR MOTHERS' GROUP

Usually in Australia your hospital will assign you a Mothers' Group. This is a group of women who have all had babies at about the same time in your local area. These women and their families will be an invaluable resource for you as they are at the same stage of life as you. They will be a great reference team for ideas and realities of what it's really like in other people's families. On that note, I find that Mothers Groups can sometimes be a bit competitive. New mums seem to obsess over *percentiles* and milestones. Don't let this stress you out. All babies are different and just because your baby is the last to walk, talk or get a tooth – doesn't mean there is anything wrong with them, or anything wrong with you. Simply, children grow and develop at different rates.

The more you meet with your group, the more you will get out of it. So if nobody else is organising anything, be the one that steps up and plans a regular catch-up. Reasons to spend time with your Mothers' Group, even if you think you don't like many (or any!) of them:

- As you spend time with them, you'll become friends with at least one
- Your Little Person will have a group of friends, from birth, who can all celebrate birthdays together
- You have a network of Big People who are going through the same battles as you at the same time. They will have a wealth of solutions and their outcomes
- They will probably go to the same schools
- You live close and will probably end up at the same parks anyway
- They become part of your team!

CHILDCARE

Even if you are sure that you aren't going to use childcare, put your name down on at least 5 different centres in your local area. Things change and the amount of effort it takes to get on the waiting list 'just in case' is worth it. These days, the best time to do this is before you even conceive. It can be nearly impossible to get into childcare without being on a waiting list, so be as prepared as you can. If you have your heart set on one place, that's fine, just give yourself a few Plan Bs. Family day care is a great option.

If your child is ready for childcare now and you haven't put your name down anywhere, an option to consider is 'occasional care'. This is a centre that takes week-by-week bookings and doesn't have permanent places.

Friends

Your group of friends will usually change significantly once you have children. It's like the change from single life to being in a couple. I know that whenever I'm in a long-term relationship, generally most of the people I spend time with are committed too. Something about going out on the town to help my single friends 'pick up' just doesn't seem fun anymore.

People with children talk about their kids all the time. Sorry, but that is you now. People without kids can, usually, only handle so much kid talk. They are in a totally different world – one with long restful nights, sleep-ins and time to lounge around reading and watching entire seasons of HBO shows in one day. For some reason you will feel compelled to talk about the colour of your kid's poo and that funny thing they said yesterday and how tired you are and ... your friend will smile and nod and be busy for the next six months. That's fine, because there are other people with kids who will delight in talking about their Little People's poo too.

Also, you may have friends that have secretly been trying to have a baby for years and find it difficult to be around your new family. Some people find Little People loud and obnoxious and can't stand having them within earshot. Some people have hundreds of precious things scattered around their house and it will be terrifying taking your little 'tornado of destruction' there. It's natural that at your new stage of life, these people may fade away into the background and new friends at a similar stage to you will become great friends. Mentally prepare yourself for the shedding of old friends and keep an eye out for all the new ones.

School friends

Your Little People will make friends at school. You then have to hang out with their parents. Sometimes this is amazing, sometimes not so much. Be prepared to be subjected to all sorts of people that you never would have met in your BC (Before Children) life.

If this isn't going so well for you, talk to the Big People you like at school pick-up and do some matchmaking play dates.

My Mum is still friends with some of my brother's primary school friends' mothers. While my brother has moved on from all those people, nearly *thirty years* later, the mums still catch up.

Nannies

Choosing the right nanny is a bit like choosing the right partner. Give yourself plenty of time to find and choose the right one. This person will become like a third parent to your Little Person, so don't feel awkward about screening them thoroughly. I would even pull out your list of questions from your partner team meeting and run through the appropriate questions with your potential nannies. You need to know things like:

- How long have they been a nanny?
- How many families have they worked with? How many children?
- Why did they leave their last job?
- How do they comfort Little People?
- How do they discipline Little People, and what for?
- Are they willing to change these things to match your style?
- What rules have and haven't worked for you in the past?
- How long do they think a baby should be left to cry?
- What would they do if the baby wouldn't stop crying?
- How would they handle a temper tantrum?
- What about rocking to sleep? Dummies? Controlled crying?
- What sort of games do they play with Little People?
- Will they do craft?
- How much screen time would they allow?
- Are they willing to do housework?
- Will they cook? For Big People or just the Littlies?
- Remember to talk about their expectations regarding pay rates, holidays, sick leave, overtime, flexible hours and late fees. (This is usually where the relationship with nannies breaks down. You must establish clear expectations around these things. Write a contract).

Ask all of the questions that are important to you. Always check several references and ask lots of questions. Use an interview to get really clear on what a nanny believes about discipline, settling and housework expectations. Make sure the nanny is on the same page as you and trust your intuition when hiring a nanny. If you hire someone and feel it isn't working out, it is okay to break up with your nanny. Have a three-month trial period – just in case.

BABYSITTERS

Hopefully you can rely on the network you have created for those times when you need a babysitter. Try to find that family that you can rely on to pick up your child from care in case of an emergency. Even organise an 'I'll pick them both up Mondays, and you do Wednesdays' system for mutual benefit.

Find out if any of your friends are interested in babysitting or ask your parents if they would like to have a sleepover.

> Another way you can stay feeling connected is to spread the love! Say nice things to others. Acknowledge the mum having a hard day. Say 'Well done' to someone with well-behaved kids next time you're out. Strangers will talk to you more openly now that you have a Little Person. Recognise these opportunities for connection, especially if you are feeling isolated. Try to make eye contact and really listen to strangers who open a dialogue. It's habit to brush off these random people who strike up a conversation. Be aware of how you receive people and connect as much as you can!

Action list:

- *Call a team meeting with your partner. Get clear on their expectations and ideas about parenting.*
- *Meet regularly with your Mothers' Group.*
- *Book into at least five childcare places ASAP even if you don't think you'll go.*
- *Be on the lookout for new friends. Have a chat with that mother you are always next to at Gymbaroo.*
- *If you need to hire a nanny, give yourself plenty of time to find the right one and trust your gut.*

3. Taking Time Out

As a parent you must, must, must take time out for yourself, your relationship and your sanity. This is a conversation I often have with parents and many argue with me. It always goes like this:

'As a parent you must, must, must take time out. Go to a yoga class, have a fortnightly date night or just spent an hour in the bath by yourself'.

'Claire that's all well and good but we can't afford a babysitter'.

Now I understand what it's like to not have excess cash but I also understand what it's like to be a little bit mental. And trust me, if you choose to take absolutely no time out you will start to behave a little bit loopy.

Let me ask you this: if you were crazy, actually clinically diagnosed with a psychological or psychiatric condition, would you be able to scrape together the $80 to see a medical practitioner? And usually those specialists aren't effective from a one-time visit so, would you be able to scrape together the $80 to return once a week/fortnight/month plus any medications you needed? I bet you would.

I'm suggesting that, instead of waiting until you go crazy and then finding the money to spend on your mental health, spend the money on prevention.

I know that your children are your biggest priority. And because you need to be there to look after them, you need to care for yourself first. Remember the oxygen on the plane? Even though you may feel selfish taking some time out for yourself, trust me it's not selfish. Being able to nurture yourself will help you to be the best parent that you can be for your Little Person. Now, book that babysitter. If you have done your 'gathering your team' homework, you might even get someone for free!

Action list:

- *Get comfortable with the idea that you need space. You can't spend every second with your Little Person.*
- *Build trusting relationships with people you can leave your Little Person with.*
- *Just do it!*
- *Remember to take time out regularly. It is for your own sanity.*

4. 'BRAIN HACKS' FOR PARENTS

POWER OF THE MIND

Our most powerful assets are in our skulls. (Unless you're in a club and the music is really loud!)

No really. The power of the mind is an incredible thing. Apparently it takes in about a million or so bits of information every second. But then our conscious mind, that never-ending commentary, only shares with us about 50 of these bits per second.

That is a serious amount of un-communication, right? Imagine if your partner only told you 0.00005% of what you needed to know! Luckily for us our conscious minds are doing us a favour because if we actually

---

processed all of that information we would explode like a grape in the microwave.

So our conscious mind will pick out what it perceives to be the relevant information for us. Luckily, *we get to choose* what bits we will look for. We can prime our brains to notice what we want, and with practice, learn to switch off our attention from the things that make us unhappy. Have you ever woken up 'on the wrong side of the bed', stubbed your toe, gone to the toilet before noticing there is no toilet paper, got a whopping unexpected bill conveniently delivered to your inbox and had the baby projectile vomit everywhere ... all before breakfast? I have, and believe me, I don't remember many positive things about that day. In fact, I don't remember anything positive. It just went on and on with the whole world seemingly against me for the entire day.

Another example is when you buy a new car, and all of a sudden you start seeing the same car everywhere! This is because your conscious mind has decided that those cars are now interesting and has stopped throwing them out with the other 999,950-ish bits of information.

Let's do an experiment. Choose something that you are going to notice today. Maybe it's yellow cars. Butterflies. Strawberry-flavoured stuff. People wearing white pants. Whatever you choose, just tell your conscious mind you'd like to see them today and watch what happens. Stop reading this book for a second, and choose something that you are going to notice today. Do it now.

So now I've got you noticing white pants or yellow cars, what does that have to do with parenting? Well, now you can transfer that skill to notice how your Little Person is doing such awesome sleeping, even if it is only for twenty minutes. You could choose to notice all the mouth-fuls that *do* get swallowed and not the two that don't. You could even notice all the quiet rustling of leaves next time your Little Person starts singing *Let It Go* for the fifty-fourth time today. And what about you? You could notice how awesome you look in your jeans. How you managed to successfully explain complicated physics in a language a toddler can understand, drive a car and do the bag scrounge to hunt for a drink for the baby, all at once. You could notice how you have trained an otherwise wild human to say *please* and *thank you* without being prompted. That is seriously cool.

The examples I have here are a little bit silly, but if you can master this skill it will make a huge difference to your self-talk. We have a habit of being *really* hard on ourselves, especially while doing new things outside of our comfort zone. Add to this, that you often don't have someone on the sidelines cheering you along the entire journey. Parenting can be a very confusing, lonely journey and this is a time when you need to be on your own team. You'll face the biggest challenges of your life with very little or no recognition for pretty much everything you do. So being able to notice all the positive things around you and choose what that voice on your head is talking about is going to be a pretty important skill.

So get clear. What do you want to notice more of? Sometimes it could be the opposite of the things you want to see less of.

Write them down and stick them up where you will see them often.

Action list:

- *Write down three great/positive things you want to notice more of.*

    1.
    2.
    3.

GRATITUDE

You cannot be grateful and bitter.
You cannot be grateful and unhappy.
You cannot be grateful and without hope.
You cannot be grateful and unloving.
So just be grateful.
            • Some unknown groover a very long time ago

Studies have shown that people who regularly practise feeling thankful have a head start when it comes to their health and happiness. Gratitude is one of the major stepping-stones that I use to shift my mindset to a more positive one.

Research has shown over and over again that those with more material possessions are just as likely to report low levels of 'life satisfaction' as someone living in poverty in India. This shows that it is not what we have that makes us happy, it is how we feel about what we have.

"I will be happy with my body as soon as I lose my baby belly" or "I'll be happy when there are no more nappies" or "I'll be happy when they grow up a bit and can amuse themselves". Thoughts like these are kind of redundant, because as soon as you lose the kilos your skin sags, you are washing ten thousand pairs of wet pants and as you do, the kids entertain themselves by drawing all over your lounge, you will be wishing for something else.

Learning to practise gratitude will help you to find joy in the little things each day. Be mindful of what you do have. Be thankful for the amazing technology of disposable nappies, your body that carries you so gracefully through this life and the magic moments you have each day with your Little People. While nothing around you has changed, shifting your perception will make it feel like it has. If you can find thankfulness for things that once bothered you, you will see a huge shift in your perception of the world. Because, "If we do not feel grateful for what we already have, what makes us think we would be happy with more?" – another unknown groover.

One of the simplest ways to be mindful of what you already have and to reframe situations as positive is to keep a gratitude journal. A place where you record a few things each day that you are grateful for. It might be a notebook by your bed, an app that bleeps at you each day or just a note on your phone. This simple activity has shown in scientific studies to make participants feel better about their lives overall, be more optimistic about the future, and report fewer health problems than the other participants. Interestingly, the participants practising daily gratitude also reported getting more sleep, spending less time awake before falling asleep and feeling more refreshed in the morning. Wow. Such a simple activity can do all that?

It's so easy; all you need to do is spend literally three minutes scribbling down some things you are grateful for. But even with the best intentions, many of us (myself included) tend to get about three days in before we forget about it. So what is stopping us from following through with activities like this one?

The biggest obstacle to having an 'attitude of gratitude' is forgetfulness and lack of awareness. You can overcome this with visual cues.

How to Be the Big Person Your Little Person Needs

Putting post it notes up is how I do this. I have little notes on the fridge, by my bed and even on the steering wheel of my car.

Another trick is to have an accountability buddy. You could have a friend that wants to start a daily journal. If not, you can convince one to! Then you hold each other accountable. I've done this for many things I am trying to get done - from exercise to work. Sometimes it's a system where we just text each other 'done' when we have completed our daily task, or send a picture of what we needed to do. You could share your gratitude list with your buddy. We are very good at breaking promises to ourselves but much less likely to do so if we promise someone else. If the idea of having a buddy doesn't sit well with you, you could make a public announcement instead. Tell your corner of the internet that you are going to complete a gratitude journal every day. Even this is enough to boost your chances of following through.

What are you grateful for right now? Maybe you are grateful that your Little Person is asleep. Maybe you are grateful for a special moment you shared today. What about people? Who are you grateful to have in your life? Tell them!

Action list:

- *Choose a place and time to fill in a Gratitude Journal every day.*
- *Write down three things you are grateful for.*

    Today I am grateful for:
    1. . . . .

    2. . . . .

    3. . . . .

GOOD VIBRATIONS

Your energetic vibration will affect your Little Person.

Your vibration is the energy your body is putting out to your immediate environment. Some people will notice their energy affects those around them. Or that their own energy is affected by other people in their space. Like when someone really cranky comes into the room, you can almost feel the prickly waves coming at you. Contrast that feeling with when a fantastic speaker delivers their speech with such passion it is contagious. You feel yourself leaning forward, listening attentively and bouncing back that enthusiastic energy.

I like to think of this like radio waves. So our emotional state and internal dialogue is the transmitter, sending invisible waves of energy out to our environment. Sometimes other people pick up on this energy. There are those that are really tuned into 'energy frequency' and are labelled intuitive or empathic. Lots of Big People are so busy creating their own radio station, they don't really notice other people's energy.

While some people aren't aware of this energy, Little People are especially sensitive to it, so let's talk about how you can modify your energy to positively influence your children's.

The first step to modifying your energetic vibration is awareness. Practising mindfulness and regularly checking in with yourself to notice how you are feeling will help you be aware.

You then need to choose a more positive feeling and focus on this.

Activity time!

Check in. How are you feeling right now? You're reading, so probably quite relaxed.

Think of a time when you were really excited. Maybe it's when you realised you were going to have a baby, or when you were about to embark on a big adventure.

Really relive that moment. Close your eyes and see it, hear it, feel it. Focus on that feeling you get in your stomach, chest or throat. That fluttering lightness of excitement. The corners of your eyes and mouth may turn up. Your breath might get a bit shallower.

If you haven't closed your eyes and done this yet, do it now!

Sometimes it can take a bit of practice to call up powerful emotions quickly. So if you found that challenging, keep practising. If it was easy, do it again by thinking of a *really sad time* in your life, and noticing the different sensations that come up. Then switch back to *excited*.

Congratulations, you have just manipulated your energetic vibration.

If you have never done an exercise like this, the feeling you are focusing on may be fleeting. With practice, you can quickly tune into different 'frequencies'. Create a collection of moments for different emotions and practise pulling these emotions to the surface on cue. Handy ones to have are calm/relaxed, happy, patient, grateful, focused and confident.

Use this skill of choosing the energetic vibration you send to your Little Person. Try to replace *anxiety* with *calm*, *despair* with *hope*. Of course this is easier said than done, but when the going gets tough, check in, and often if you can change your energy, things revolutionise.

When settling your child it is really important to be aware of your vibration. If you are frazzled and skittish, your Little Person will pick up on that and mirror that energy. That will make it especially difficult for them to get to sleep.

When I am settling Little People to sleep I make a real effort to slow my thoughts, leave my To-Do list outside the door and slow my breathing. I try to breathe like a sleeping baby would. Deep, slow breaths. If I'm patting a child to sleep I close my eyes, relax every muscle I can and pretend I am asleep too.

(Another tip, if you are patting a baby to sleep, use a random tune rather than a consistent beat. A slow version of *Old MacDonald* works a treat, but why not try your favourite song?)

Highly strung Big People usually have highly strung Little People in tow, so try to keep your breathing slow and relaxed and smile lots!

Action list:

- *Choose three emotions that empower you (happy, excited, etc.)*
- *Find a memory where that emotion was strong*
- *Use that memory as a gateway to practise dialling up that emotion*
- *Get excited for no real reason! Actively change the way you feel*

5. SETTING GOALS

People who are successful in achieving what they put their mind to, set goals and review them regularly. When I learnt this, I decided to spend some time getting clear on my goals and wrote down some SMART goals. If you haven't heard of SMART goals here is a quick outline. Goals must be:

- **Specific** – they must be clear
- **Measurable** – they must be quantifiable
- **Actionable** – they must be capable of being acted on
- **Realistic** – they must be achievable
- **Time bound** – they need to have deadlines

So I wrote myself some SMART goals, typed them up and printed them with some matching images I found on Google. I needed to put these goals somewhere I would see them a lot, so I stuck them on the ceiling above my bed. As I go to sleep I am thinking about how this financial year I am going to double my income from last financial year. And as I wake up I am reminded to start the *daily actions* that will get me to that place. While I have some massive goals on my ceiling, I also have great day-to-day reminders of the person I want to be, and the things that I know make me happy/keep me sane. My ceiling reminds me to meditate every day and how I feel when I do that. It reminds me to take care of myself by doing yoga twice a week and to do more than I am asked to do at least once a day.

The whole exercise took me about an hour and, through reviewing my goals regularly I am achieving amazing things in short timeframes, while also filling my life with more awareness, compassion and mindfulness.

With Little People around we often forget to do these things and end up living in their moment-to-moment emotionally-fuelled worlds. We can get lost in a blur of sleep-deprived weeks and the biggest thing to celebrate is the fact that the dishes got done. Keeping focused on goals makes a massive difference to Big People's mindset. It can change the way we spend our days and leave us feeling like we have really achieved something.

So what can you do to make your days feel more like little achievements and less like a jumbled-up To-Do list that has no real outcome?

Set some SMART goals. Post them somewhere you will see them every day. It doesn't have to be the ceiling above your bed. Just have them front and centre somewhere. Maybe your bathroom mirror, a post-it by your toothbrush, on the fridge or stuck to the coffee tin. Make them relevant to your life at home, not just long-term and financial goals. You could start with things like:

- I will finish reading that novel I started last year by October
- I will teach my Little Person ten colours by 30th May
- I will do a YouTube yoga class once a week during naptime
- I will start the day with a healthy breakfast every day for 30 days
- When I feel frustrated, I will count to 10 instead of yelling this week
- On Fridays, I will win the laundry battle, and at the weekends I will enjoy being on laundry strike. *Every week!*

How to Be the Big Person Your Little Person Needs

You get the idea. Not all goals need to be career or money focused. It may seem strange, but try to set some goals for things that you are already doing. This will make you feel like you are making headway and that your days are more than just nappy changes and singing *The wheels on the bus* on loop.

The next part to this exercise is to justify to yourself *why* achieving each goal is important to you. This is a crucial step because it creates a link between your goals and your desires, and if you don't desire the outcome enough, you will not achieve your goal. And finally, you need to give yourself a road map to break down the actions you need to take to get to your goal.

Why not get started right now?

SMART Goal	By:	How?	Why?
E.g.: Win the laundry battle. Have nothing that needs washing for one glorious moment in time on a Friday evening.	Every Friday by 10pm.	Do one load each day. Towels- Monday, whites- Tuesday, colours- Wednesday, tea towels etc.- Thursday and whatever leftovers that need doing on Friday. Over the weekend wet pants can go in a bucket.	So I can spend my weekends with my family and have some much deserved 'time off' from being the laundry lady (or man).

Once you have written down your SMART goals, you will find that you can break many of them down into daily/weekly/monthly tasks. Before you go to bed each night, scribble out a quick To-Do list for the next day. I find great satisfaction in scratching things off a list. It helps me to feel like I am achieving something and there is a purpose to my life – other than meeting Little People's needs.

This 'chunking down' is especially important if you have big goals. Getting fit is a great example of a big goal. It takes time and consistent commitment. The secret to staying committed to long term goals is letting yourself feel like you are making progress. So I stop to celebrate *every time* I finish a workout or a healthy meal.

A daily To-Do list will be very different for each of us, depending on our goals, but here is an example:

1. Wash the whites
2. Earn $200
3. Go for a 20 minute jog
4. Eat two cups of green leafy vegetables
5. If frustrated, I will count to ten

A list like this has the power to transform your day into one that brings you closer to your long term goals, instead of just another 24 hour block.

If you can visualise yourself achieving these goals it will help your brain to get really focused on what you want. Remember, your brain speaks in pictures. Earlier in the book, in chapter two you practised pushing vivid thoughts away when you are anxious. For goal setting and things you want to make real in your life you do the opposite of that exercise. So you visualise yourself achieving your goals in full vivid colour. Make the image big and close and loud in your mind. And remember to see it as if through your own eyes. If you are watching yourself in a movie it tells your brain it isn't real.

Action list:

- *Write some SMART goals*
- *Double check that each goal has a deadline*
- *Break them down into manageable tasks*
- *Write a mindful To-Do list each night*
- *Achieve stuff and reward yourself!*

6. Mindfulness

Often when I tell people what I do, they say something like, "Wow that must be so exhausting" or "Ugh, toddlers all day every day. You must be so patient!"

Maybe I am a bit more patient than some people, but I can tell you that is no accident. I have spent many years cultivating mindfulness and meditation. Practising mindfulness is said to improve well-being, physical health, mental health and relationships. Here is a list of some of the ways a little bit of mindfulness can affect your life.

Being mindful helps you:
- relieve stress (and what parent isn't stressed?)
- to experience more calm and peacefulness
- worry less about the future or past

- connect with others
- avoid becoming or staying depressed
- sleep better
- savour pleasures in life as they occur
- be fully engaged in activities
- have a greater capacity to deal with unpleasant events
- feel generally more satisfied with life
- accept your experiences
- be fully present, here and now
- experience unpleasant thoughts and feelings in safety
- become aware of things you're avoiding
- become more connected to yourself, to others and to the world around you
- have more direct contact with the world, rather than living through your thoughts
- learn that everything changes; that thoughts and feelings come and go like the weather
- have more balance and less emotional volatility
- be more self-aware
- develop self-acceptance and self-compassion
- but most importantly, *it helps you to parent the way you want to, rather than just reacting to your Little People.*

That is a pretty long list of things it would be nice to master! So how can you do it?

There are many different ways to practise mindfulness, but the aim is to achieve a state of alert, focused relaxation by paying attention to thoughts and sensations without judging yourself. This allows your mind to focus on the present moment. All mindfulness techniques are a form of meditation.

Here are some ways that you can practise being more mindful:

Basic mindfulness meditation – Sit quietly and focus on your breathing or on a word or *mantra* that you repeat silently. You might just say to yourself: *inhale, exhale, inhale, exhale* as you breathe. Allow thoughts to come and go. This is a tricky thing to do. Think of these thoughts that pop up as cars cruising by. Let them continue along the road, don't run into the street and flag them down.

When you notice you are caught up in a thought, celebrate that you noticed and return your focus to your breath or mantra.

There are some great resources on YouTube. Just search 'five minute mindfulness'.

Body sensations – Notice subtle body sensations such as an itch or tingling without reacting and let them pass. Notice each part of your body. Start with your toes, feet ankles, calves, knees, thighs, and so on.

Sensory – My favourite mindfulness exercise is a game called *Take Five*. Stop and check in with: (in fact, do this one right now)
- Five things you can see
- Four things you can hear
- Three things you can feel
- Two things you can smell.
- One thing you can taste

Emotions – Practise checking in and recognising what you're feeling. Name the emotion. Don't beat yourself up for feeling that way or try to change it. Just sit in it and be mindful.

Try a few different ways to be mindful. There are plenty of other ways to stop and take note. Find one or two that really work for you and practise them!

Set up triggers that will remind you to pause and be mindful. It might be when you eat, you really notice the tastes and sensations (a great one if you are prone to overeating). It might be as your Little Person tells you about their day you stop, get down to their level (eye-to-eye) and really listen; or it could be every time you get into a lift, you just stop and pay attention to your breath. Make it easy for yourself.

Action list:

- *If you haven't already, spend five minutes, right now, try one of the mindfulness techniques*
- *Do a search for 'five minute mindfulness' on YouTube*
- *Next time you are waiting for something, somewhere like a waiting room, bus stop or even an elevator, play the 'Take Five' game*
- *Commit to a regular mindfulness practice. Be realistic. While daily would be ideal, it's important to be realistic. Set some smart goals, and schedule your new practice. If you don't make*

a time, it won't happen
- *Practise makes perfect. So practise!*

Note: For meditation, I use an app called Headspace. I highly recommend it. Check out the creator, Andy Puddicombe's TED talk called: *All it takes is 10 mindful minutes.*

Part II: Little People

Okay so part one was all about you and creating a strong foundation by looking after yourself first. You learned some ways to look after your body and mind, your social network, and your mindset. This next part of the book is dedicated to recognising and explaining the fundamentals of child rearing. There are seven keys to having well-behaved, happy children. These concepts are quite simple, yet regularly forgotten. Not anymore though, as I have created the seven ABCs to having toddlers that thrive. So all you have to remember is ABC!

Remember our apple tree? In part one you have gained some skills that represent your roots. Now you are ready for part two, your trunk. At first it might be spindly and narrow, but with time it will strengthen to be the anchor for your fruit. I suggest you take some time to really implement each of these seven ABCs. Often one or two will be very effective, but when all seven come together you will find your toddler will really thrive.

Have you ever wondered how that mother of four can happily navigate the world with her seemingly, perfectly-behaved children? This part is the answer. Or maybe you want to know how Childcare workers can manage 10 babies under two, for 10 hours straight, every day for 20 years and be the coolest, calm and collected ladies on the planet? Read on.

Little People feel most comfortable when their Big People are providing them with the keys outlined in the following pages. If they sense weakness in their Big Person it can often lead to a battle for control. Children *will* test you on these seven ABCs. They do this because they find comfort in knowing what their boundaries are, and only know for sure where they stand once they have tested and found the limits.

If Big People come unstuck on any one of these fundamental concepts, their attempts to make big changes to Little People's behaviour could do more harm than good. Be warned: until you are sure that you are practising all of these concepts, not just thinking about it, you must not begin the specific techniques from part three. If you begin attempting to retrain your toddler to self-settle before you have nailed the – often very challenging – art of follow through, you will be in danger of making your life so much harder. The execution of the behaviour-change techniques (in part three) requires Big People that really understand and con-sistently use these seven fundamentals. Spend at least a few days on each chapter (even if the concept seems simple), implement the action lists and watch your Little Person blossom. Remember knowledge without action is futile.

So, let's get started!

7. The ABCs that Every Little Person Needs to Keep the Sh...ugar from Hitting the Fan

I have created an easy-to-remember set of ABCs for you. Again, some of these concepts will seem quite simple but I encourage you to really check in on your skills and make sure you are confident before you start testing yourself.

The better you are at doing these things day to day when it doesn't really matter, the more likely it is you will succeed with the techniques later in the book, the first time, with the minimum amount of fuss for everyone.

Are you ready? The magic ingredients are:

- **A** - A Routine
- **B** - Boundaries
- **C** - Consistency
- **D** - Discipline
- **E** - Environment
- **F** - Follow through
- **G** - Gratitude.

So, let's stack the odds in your corner and master these skills!

8. A is for A Routine

It's no mistake school bells ring at 9, 11, 1 and 3. Children are happiest when they know what is coming next and how long they have to finish what they are doing. The bodies of children work in cycles and if you can meet their needs before they lose the plot, life becomes much more peaceful. Tired and hungry Little People are not happy Little People.

Many children these days begin their lives being demand-fed and sleeping when they choose rather than when you would like. This is all well and good until you have a three year old that has never slept through the night. At some point, the Little Person needs a Big Person to take the reins and start controlling their environment. Many people start strict routines practically from birth, and others choose to let their toddler dictate, hoping they will just *grow out of it*. I would opt for something in the middle. By three to six months your Little Person is definitely ready for someone to start helping them get into a routine.

A small side note here on 'growing out of it'. While I may be biased as I see many of the worst-case scenarios, I think it is very rare that a Little Person will just 'grow out' of things like night-time wake-ups and food refusal. We need to actually *do something* to change the situation.

A routine is invaluable, especially with really Little People, as it allows them to have their needs met, before they end up screaming, to tell you they need something. It also helps to keep Big People much calmer as they know when to expect to feed, settle and sometimes even change their Little Person. (Gotta love those regular pooers.)

It means that your outings can be planned between nap and meal times and you will almost never have a Little Person that is screaming. This is because they don't reach that state of over-tiredness or starvation. You have met those needs in advance, because you as the Big Person could predict them.

Older toddlers thrive in a routine too. Being control freaks they really need to know what is coming next well in advance. If you can set out the day to be as predictable as possible for your Little Person, you will have fewer battles. You will find yourself singing out, 'It's bedtime' at 6:55pm and when confronted with a 'Why?' you will come back with 'Because we just had books and after we read books – it's bedtime'. To which your Little Person will say 'Oh, okay' as they tuck themselves in.

SO WHAT IS A ROUTINE?

A routine is a plan with a sequence of actions that is followed regularly. In relation to Little People it is usually a schedule of sleep, meal and play times.

WHY ARE ROUTINES IMPORTANT?

Routines are important because they help you to keep your Little Person happy, their needs met and create a sense of comfort for them.

How can you set solid routines?

If you have a Little Person that is currently demand-feeding and sleeping, keep a record of what is currently happening for at least one week. (There is a place to do that coming up). Then shop around and see if you can find a routine that looks similar to what your Little Person is already doing. You will find some ideas on the following pages, but if they don't seem right for you, I urge you to have a look online, ask your Mothers' Group or create your own.

Use the routine as a *guideline* for an ideal day. Some Big People are frightened of routines because they have a friend that raves about them like they are in some cult. They are obsessed with the time and always have to be home at thirteen minutes to one for sleep time. I'm not asking you to join that cult. Use the routine to predict your Little Person's needs before they become overdue, make plans in advance around what will probably be happening food/sleep-wise and to troubleshoot why your Little Person is stroppy.

Just when you have a routine down pat, be prepared to have your Little Person change the rules and require a new one.

Record what your Little Person does for at least a week:

Here is an example of what this might look like:

7:10 – woke
7:25 – milk feed
8:00 – mush
8:20 – play
9:30 – fell asleep on the floor
9:34 – woke up when put into bed
9:35 – screamed
9:40 – into stroller, still screaming
9:44 – asleep, but only until stroller stops moving.

(I'm being silly, but you get the idea. Track sleep and wake times, milk feeds and solids).

You could use this chart:

TIME	EAT	DRINK	POO	PLAY	SLEEP	UPSET	CALM
7:00							
7:15							
7:30							
7:45							
8:00							
8:15							
8:30							
8:45							
9:00							
9:15							
9:30							
9:45							
10:00							
10:15							
10:30							
10:45							
11:00							
11:15							
11:30							
11:45							
12:00							
12:15							
12:30							
12:45							
1:00							
1:15							
1:30							
1:45							
2:00							
2:15							
2:30							

How to Be the Big Person Your Little Person Needs

2:45							
3:00							
3:15							
3:30							
3:45							
4:00							
4:15							
4:30							
4:45							
5:00							
5:15							
5:30							
5:45							
6:00							
6:15							
6:30							
6:45							
7:00							
7:15							
7:30							
7:45							
8:00							

From the data you have collected above, you will be able to piece together a tailored routine for your Little Person. I have created a general
guideline for those of you that haven't done your homework. It is the
kind of routine your little person would be moulded into if they were to
start at a Childcare centre. These sleep and meal times are very typical at
Childcare, (which is good to know before you start at one). The routine
includes all ages from three months to school age because I don't know
how old your Little People are. If you need something more specific to
your Little Person's age group, or if they are under three months of age
then Google can definitely help with that. I have found that Tizzie Hall's
routines have been pretty spot on for the babies that I have worked with.
While I found many parts of her 'Save our sleep' book quite confronting
and disagree with much of her message, her routines are great. So here
is the guideline:

7.00 Wake up.

7.30 Breakfast

8.00 Indoor/outdoor play, craft, dancing, singing, book, musical instruments

9.00 Milk feed (for 3-12 month olds)

9.15 Wash hands and morning tea

9.30 Sleep time for under 12 month olds

9.30 Indoor/outdoor play, craft, dancing, singing, book, musical instruments, structured class

11.15 Wash hands and lunch

11.45 Sleep for 12 months and over

12.30 Indoor/outdoor play, craft, dancing, singing, book, musical instruments for 3-12 month olds

2.15 Wash hands, afternoon tea or milk feed

2.30 Sleep time for under 12 month olds

3.00 Free indoor/outdoor play, craft, dancing, singing, book, musical instruments

4.00 Drink and fruit

4.45 Free indoor/outdoor play

5.30 Dinner or milk feed

6.00 Bath

6.20 Milk feed for 3-12 months

6.30 Bedtime wind down cuddles, books, brush teeth, quiet activities

7.00 Bed

Action list:

- By 3-6 months, start helping your Little Person get into a routine
- Plan outings between nap and meal times
- Make toddlers' days predictable
- Keep a record of that is happening for one week
- Piece together a tailored routine for your Little Person. Use the guidelines if you need to.

9. B IS FOR BOUNDARIES

Children are most comfortable when they know exactly where their boundaries are. Inside those boundaries is their safe zone to live and play. They will regularly test these boundaries and feel comforted when they find them. If they can't find solid, 150% reliable limits to what is acceptable they will continue to push and test, seeking them. This is hard work for them and even harder for you.

Think of boundaries like a circle. If we have done a good job of establishing consistent boundaries for our Little People they know exactly how big their circle is.

You will notice that if a child finds a shaky boundary in one area of their circle, they will do a perimeter check and test all the other boundaries to make sure the rest of their limits haven't changed. So, if you think it's simpler to just give in on a battle, be prepared to have many of your *other* limits tested in the coming days.

Imagine you are on a sailing boat that has no safety rails. The boat is on a 45° angle as it skips across the water bouncing over the waves. How do you feel? If you're anything like me, you'd be as far from the edges as possible, flat against the deck, clutching at anything you can get a good grip on.

Now what if I installed some strong, sturdy safety rails around the edges of the boat? A clear boundary between where you are and the deep, dark, fast-moving ocean. Now how do you feel? I feel much more secure. In fact, I'd probably walk around the boat now, and as I got more confident I'd probably even venture over to the edge to sit with my legs hanging out over the water. I feel safe and supported by my boundaries and enjoy the whole experience of sailing much more!

This is what it is like for Little People in the big unknown world. They need you to construct boundaries for them to keep them safe and let them know where they can explore without hurting themselves or those around them.

There are rules and boundaries scattered everywhere in our lives. A particularly clear boundary is 'drive on the left side of the road'. This means we are safe and traffic flows better. A less tangible example: we are allowed to take a certain amount of sick days from work, if we take any more then our employer requires a Doctor's Certificate. If excessive sick leave is taken, the time off work will likely be unpaid. There is another boundary when we have taken so many days off work that it means that we may not have a job to go back to.

A great illustration of how boundaries and rules can be beneficial for Little People can be found in sports.

Last week I heard the story of a father who took his daughter to her weekly soccer training. Her normal coach wasn't there and the whole team was looking around waiting for someone to start the game. Luckily one of the dads was feeling brave so he fronted up and got the girls playing. While everyone was grateful that he was having a crack, he didn't really know the rules or how to coach 6 year olds to play soccer. The result was total chaos. The kids were crashing into each other, crying and fighting all over the place! But when the actual coach turned up, he gave the girls their positions, outlined the rules and reminded them what their boundaries were. What an incredible difference that made!

The chaotic disaster turned into a smooth game, which allowed the girls to actually have fun.

SO WHAT DOES IT MEAN TO HAVE BOUNDARIES?

Having boundaries means that there are limits to what your child can be, do and have.

Some of these boundaries will be there to keep them safe. Some will be to keep you sane. Many will be for the consideration of others in their environment. There are age appropriate limitations, height restrictions and sometimes, just flat-out rules.

Here is an example. When Ben was two and a half he moved from a cot to a big bed. He was very excited about this because he could get up and leave whenever he felt like it! Luckily his mother had worked with me and knew how important boundaries are. She resolved to nip this Jack-in-the-box bedtime game in the bud. Starting from the very first day she explained to Ben that he wasn't to come downstairs after bedtime. Of course Ben didn't listen, and whenever he came downstairs his mother would promptly take him back up to bed. Ben was quick to catch on that the stairs were the boundary. He ended up falling asleep at the top of the stairs. His mother found him there with one leg and one arm hanging over the top step and a little wet patch in the carpet from where he had been wailing. He knew the exact place of the boundary. While he played inside the lines he still needed two limbs over the edge just to rebel.

If you are worried about Ben and his wailing I'd like to take a minute to explain why this was the best method for this particular child in this particular circumstance. Ben is an incredibly strong-willed child who takes fifteen miles when given an inch. The stress for him of learning this unwavering boundary lasted two nights. If however his mother had had inconsistent boundaries (altered by her emotions) and dragged out the process, sometimes letting him stay up and fall asleep on the couch downstairs, sometimes staying with him in his room, sometimes putting him in her bed, or giving him a bottle to get to sleep, Ben would have been much more stressed throughout this process. The longer, more confusing method would have created so much more stress for both mother and child. The tears accumulated over the time would have created a much bigger wet patch!

WHY ARE BOUNDARIES IMPORTANT?

When you know where you stand, you will know what you will and will not put up with from your child. You really need to know this if you are going to be consistent in the messages you send your children about what is acceptable and when they have crossed a line with you.

Having pre-determined boundaries will help you to stick to your principles rather than reacting to emotions. Emotionally-driven discipline can be confusing and lead to guilt later.

Children will encounter boundaries in play centres, at pre-school and of course at school. Understanding and respecting boundaries is an essential life skill.

They will learn to negotiate the boundaries of their peers and communicate their own boundaries with the world. We need to teach them these skills and the best way to do that is by example.

Our limits teach them to set limits for themselves. By setting boundaries we are encouraging self-discipline and control, respect for others, love and freedom.

HOW CAN YOU SET BOUNDARIES?

I often work with families with Jack-in-the-box settling routines. I need to retrain these children to stay in bed instead of getting up and playing games with their parents' sanity. When doing this we need to set boundaries that are glowing neon for the children. They are confused and need to know what is expected of them. Depending on the situation this is usually a physical boundary. Something like a doorway, sometimes as soon as their weight shifts off the mattress. Once they reach that point, it's back to bed.

When you go somewhere, make an effort to tell (or even better, show) your Little People where the physical boundaries are.

Always provide a reason for the boundary being where it is, especially if there is a safety reason. Talk to them in an adult way about what the hazard is, and describe the injury consequence in a way that makes them take notice. Keep it short though. Long-winded safety speeches go in one ear and out the other.

Take time to explain your expectations and what will happen if these are or aren't met. Use language like: 'When we go into Grandma's house,

I need you to stay in the lounge room with me. If you try to leave the room, you will have to sit on my knee'.

When a child reaches a boundary make sure you let them know. For Littlies a firm 'Ah, ah' communicates clearly. Older children understand longer explanations.

Action list:

- *Make an effort to tell (or even better, show) your Little People where the physical boundaries are*
- *Always provide a reason for the boundary being where it is, especially if there is a safety reason*
- *When a child reaches a boundary make sure you let them know*

10. C is for Consistency

Being a Little Person is all about learning. We come into the world with eyes that can't focus and limbs that flail and hit us in the face. Slowly but surely, through trial and error we learn to control and manipulate our bodies so we can crawl, walk and even dance. We learn this through getting the same result every time we try something. We learn to gauge actions and reactions and use this knowledge to make informed decisions. When raising children, we, as Big People need to be as consistent as the firing of a muscle.

Being inconsistent will confuse your Little Person and make your boundaries blurry.

You may have seen Supernanny on TV. It's no secret that I love Jo Frost and the main reason I think she is so fantastic is her core message: consistency. Everything about that woman is consistent. She has the same message, delivered in the same format with the same results over and over again.

So what does it mean to 'be consistent'?

To be consistent means that your rules, expectations and outcomes are the same from one time to the next. Consistency helps to keep a Little Person from worrying about what might happen and makes their world predictable and less confusing.

Consistency also teaches Little People consequences for their actions.

Why is consistency important?

Consistency reinforces boundaries that give children a sense of security. It allows them to stop experimenting with behaviours and feel confident that they know what will happen as a consequence of their choices.

Consistent Big People promote confident Little People. Inconsistency leads to Little People feeling anxious.

Consistency teaches Little People consequences for their actions.

Consistency promotes peace! Testing behaviour, temper tantrums, arguments and bargaining will just fall away.

If Big People say *no means no*, and follow through with *no* consistently, Little People quickly learn that no *actually* means no. Then they are much less likely to push the limits.

Inconsistent Big People can cause confusion, poor self-esteem and negative self-values in Little People.

How can you be consistent?

Get together and set some rules. Start with just a few so everyone can keep up, write them down and stick them somewhere you will all see them. Decide as a family what the consequences for breaking the rules will be and get ready to follow through.

Only set fair rules with logical consequences *all* Big People are willing to enforce. Every. Single. Time.

Be aware of other Big People. Little People will search for the person that will say *Yes* when everyone else says *No*. This is very frustrating for those who are doing the right thing and are then seen as the Bad Guy.

How to Be the Big Person Your Little Person Needs

It also un-stitches any progress made towards a consistent message.

Remember to be consistent with positive reinforcement as well as consequences. Find techniques that fit with your family and make sure you finish them.

Some days this will be really hard. When it seems easier to just let something slide, remember that inconsistency is encouraging your Little Person to push boundaries and test your limits!

One of my most powerful sentences when guiding Little People is: 'If you _____, then _____ will happen'. The reason this is so powerful is because once those words leave my lips, they are Gospel. Whatever I have said will happen, happens. This means that the next time I outline an action and a consequence, the Little Person will trust me.

Many parents make the mistake of thinking that the threat of something happening should be enough and very rarely follow through. This doesn't work because the children no longer trust you or believe that the consequence will happen.

For example, I worked with a family that had major issues at bedtime. The battle would start at about 7:30 every night and often go until after 10pm. When I came to do an observation of what was happening at bedtime, I stood outside the door, listening to the bedtime story. It was absolute chaos. The children were running riot. Jumping and squealing, climbing all over the dad and completely ignoring his effort to read to them. He kept saying, 'Get into your beds, or I won't read you this story!' I counted those words 13 *times* before he actually put the book down. Then there was another 6, 'You need to stay in your bed or I am going to leave' before he left. These kids were desperate for consistent boundaries. It was so exhausting for everyone to have the limits being constantly tested!

These kids then went into the classic Jack-in-the-box bedtime extravaganza. They would come running from the bedroom and squeal with delight when a Big Person came chasing them down the hall. This turned into hours of fun. My favourite part was when Little Miss Four asked for some water, so her Big Person took her some. She threw a complete wobbly and demanded *different water*. And guess what. She got it delivered.

I helped this family work with these seven ABCs and they had incredible results. Power battles became a thing of the past. Even in the first few days, the teachers at Kindy and their grandparents commented on how much better their behaviour was!

Action list:

- Get together and set some rules. Start with just a few so everyone can keep up
- Write them down and stick them somewhere you will all see them
- Decide as a family what the consequences for breaking the rules will be and get ready to follow through
- Say: 'If you _____, then _____ will happen' and follow through
- Only set rules and consequences all Big People are willing to enforce. Every. Single. Time.

11. D IS FOR DISCIPLINE

Parent first, friend second

• My Illustrator

Sometimes being the 'Bad Guy' and dishing out discipline is really hard and other times it comes far too quickly – while we are frustrated or in a rage. Finding the balance between being too soft and being the *Trunchbull* (from Matilda) is a skill that takes time and practice to develop. (If you haven't seen or read Roald Dahl's *Matilda,* you should put that on your action list!)

My Mum has always let my brother and I make our own choices in life. When we were little I remember her standing aside as we ran headlong for something that would surely equal trouble and she would calmly raise one eyebrow and say, 'Actions and consequences ...' That's all she had to say. This would have us screeching on our brakes, re-evaluating our choice and what the consequences would be. Surely, it couldn't be good if she was doing the eyebrow thing!

Somewhere between the outlawing of smacking and the introduction of touch screens, something has gone missing.

I believe this something is the 'D' word. Discipline. Children *need* discipline, and I have seen way too many children who are suffering because they haven't been taught how to manage their own behaviour, through being disciplined. And you know who is suffering too, right? The Big People.

But before we delve too far here, let me just take some time to define discipline. 'Actions and consequences' – as my Mother used to say. Discipline is what we, as the Big People, need to use to train our Little People. It is the flip-side of positive reinforcement. It is the clear message that a boundary has been overstepped. There is much discussion in my field about the difference between discipline and punishment. I believe the difference is a perception that 'punishment' is seen to be cruel and punitive while discipline is seen to be more empathic and designed to teach children to manage their own behaviour.

It is time for a revival of *consequences* for negative behaviour in children. I've chosen the word *discipline* as it originally stems from the word disciple – which means to teach. (And it conveniently starts with the letter d!)

SO WHAT DOES IT MEAN TO DISCIPLINE?

To discipline means to teach your Little Person what negative behaviour is by meeting this behaviour with a negative consequence. There are five different types of consequences you can use to discipline your child:

How to Be the Big Person Your Little Person Needs

- Feeling-based consequences
- Natural consequences
- Action-reaction consequences
- Removing attention as a consequence
- Final straw consequences

THE FIVE DIFFERENT TYPES OF DISCIPLINE

1. *Feeling-based consequences* are a great form of discipline. They provide a negative consequence while teaching your Little Person about emotions and how their behaviour affects those around them.

   The formula for this one is:
   - 'When you _____ it makes me/us/them feel _____ '

   Some examples of this would be:
   - When you take the baby's toy, it makes him feel sad.
   - When you ignore me when I am calling you, it makes me feel frightened because I'm not sure if you're safe.
   - When you throw your food on the floor, it makes me feel sad and a little bit angry. It took me a long time to make that for you, and now I have to put it in the bin'

   If you do lots of this as your Little Person grows up, you will eventually be able to say, 'How would you feel if the baby snatched your toy? What could you do instead?' Empathy is a learned skill, and this form of discipline will encourage Little People to begin thinking of others and how they feel.

2. *Natural consequences* often do the work for you. So instead of nagging your Little Person about getting hurt or not eating their dinner, warn them, then let the Universe do its action–reaction thing. But be there to comfort and explain to your Little Person afterwards. Remind them that you warned them that this would happen and use this moment to build trust in your relationship. What you say actually happens! Your toddler thinks, "Wow, this Big Person knows stuff about stuff. Maybe I will listen to their warnings in future". To use this one you say:
   - 'If you _____ then _____'.

Some examples of this would be:

- If you pull the cat's tail, it will scratch you.
- If you don't eat your breakfast you will be really hungry later.

Once you have warned your Little Person, let them chose their own actions and maybe they will get scratched. While in the short term there will be a little pain/discomfort/embarrassment for your Little Person, it will be a very powerful moment of learning. Your Little Person will learn that you know stuff, and that what you say is true. They will learn to hear and trust your warnings to avoid pain.

There are times when it isn't safe to let your child learn things the hard way, so know when and where to use this form of *natural consequences* discipline.

3. *Action-Reaction consequences* are where you outline a logical negative consequence *created by you* for unwanted behaviour. This is very similar to the natural consequences outlined above. The difference is that the outcome is created by you, not 'the Universe'. This technique is usually the most effective discipline when a *logical negative consequence* is offered for negative behaviour on a case-by-case basis. In an Action-Reaction model, think about what is an appropriate, *logical* consequence for the behaviour your child is engaging in.

   Here are some examples:

   - Toby runs away at the supermarket.

     Warn Toby: You can walk, but you must hold onto the stroller. If you let go of the stroller, you will need to hop back in. (Set a clear boundary).

   - Ella keeps leaving the table during meals.

     Warn Ella: If you leave the table again, you will need to sit in your highchair instead.

   - Daniel isn't putting his shoes on after being asked.

     Warn Daniel: If you can't concentrate with the television on, I'll turn it off so you can focus on your shoes.

   This is the technique I use eighty percent of the time. Why? Because it's simple, practical, logical, you can use it anywhere for practically anything. Sometimes it takes a bit of creativity, but usually it's pretty straightforward.

4. *Removing Attention* is a successful strategy because one of the

things your Little Person values most is your attention and the attention of others. Removing attention is very effective for annoying and some types of inappropriate behaviour. If you remove attention for a negative behaviour, you *must* then reward the opposite positive behaviour *instantly* with lots of attention and acknowledgement. This instant reward of attention for the right behaviour is the key to this technique working. Notice what you do like, tell them, tell them, and tell them again.

5. Finally, for behaviour that is unsafe, harmful to others or ongoing testing behaviour, there needs to be a *final straw*. This is a very clear, *strong* consequence that is designed to quickly reform Little People's behaviour. Reserved for particularly challenging or unsafe behaviour this form of discipline requires balance and is often over- or under-used.

I will delve further into examples and strategies for this one later in the book. First we need to talk about following through!

WHY IS DISCIPLINE IMPORTANT?

Children don't come with built-in ideas of what *is* and *isn't* appropriate in our society. It is our job as Big People to teach them the skills necessary to become a responsible adult. Good discipline will help your child to learn to make better choices, manage their anxiety and other emotions, and train them to be aware and considerate of others.

HOW CAN YOU DISCIPLINE YOUR LITTLE PERSON EFFECTIVELY?

The first step is to be clear on your values and boundaries on what is – and isn't – okay to give your Little Person a very clear message that they have overstepped the line.

Give *one* clear warning of what will happen if your Little Person behaves (or continues to behave) in a certain way. Then – follow through. More than one warning will turn you into a nag, making it hard to be consistent and confusing your child about when you will or won't follow through.

If your child is violent or puts themselves in harm's way (biting and running onto the road are examples), forget the warning and make sure they know a boundary has been crossed. Remember to explain to them what they did wrong and why it was dangerous or unacceptable.

What to do:

- Identify inappropriate behaviour and choose an appropriate consequence. Make sure it is something that you are willing to follow through with, that isn't going to be another battle
- Warn the Little Person *once*. If you _____ then _____ will happen
- If the child continues, follow through with what you said you were going to do
- Move on. Talk about something else. Do something fun
- Sometimes we Big People have a habit of stewing on stuff. Let it go and get on with your day

What not to do:

- Give a second (or third, or fourth) warning
- Negotiate
- Ignore behaviour once you have already given a warning
- Get angry. There is no need to yell and stomp about. Let the consequence alone work its magic. The idea is that this *situation* will teach your child, so that future behaviour will be different

There are some fantastic techniques for different types of discipline in part three. Check the chapters Negative reinforcement, (which has information on attention removal) and 'Final straw' if you need ideas for discipline. Remember though, these techniques will do more harm than good if you don't apply the fundamental ABCs from this part first. (Especially setting clear boundaries, being consistent and following through.) Because any discipline without follow through is going to do more harm than good.

Action list:

- *Get clear on you and your partner's values and boundaries on what is – and isn't – acceptable behaviour*
- *Give one clear warning of what will happen if your Little Person behaves (or continues to behave) in a certain way*
- *Then – follow through*
- *Be prepared. Choose which of the five types of discipline will work best for you. Maybe choose a couple*

- *Stick reminders up for yourself. Things like:*
  - o *One warning*
  - o *If you _____ then _____ will happen*
  - o *'When you _____ it makes me/us/them feel _____'*
- *Once you have completed part two check the chapters 'Negative reinforcement', (which has information on attention removal) and 'Final straw' if you need ideas for discipline.*

12. E is for Environment

Within Environment, there are two equally important ingredients. One is *encouragement*, and the other is *engagement*. Let's start with encouragement, which is the flip-side to discipline, (think positive reinforcement). Discipline and negative consequences alone aren't enough to change children's behaviours. The fastest, most effective way to get a child behaving the way we want them to is to tell them what we *do* want.

Imagine you have just started a new job. You sit down at your desk, not too sure what to do. You turn on your computer and look around hoping someone will come and tell you what to do, but they don't. So, you figure instead of just sitting there, you will go and ask someone what you should be doing.

Suddenly the boss comes out and starts yelling at you because you left your desk, you haven't opened the morning e-mail they sent and you are wearing the wrong colour socks.

How do you feel? What if the boss had told you, 'On your first day, I have a meeting until 9.30, but I will come and see you as soon as I'm done. While you wait, check your e-mail, it will have a list of things you can start on. Oh and we wear blue socks around here, make sure you get yourself some'.

Seems logical, right? Be aware that children often don't know what is expected of them, and while it seems obvious to us, sometimes we forget that they are pretty new to this place called Earth. Giving them a clear outline of what we do want, and then acknowledging that behaviour will make life easier and calmer for both you and your Little People.

When your Little Person does what you have asked, you need to let them know that they have made you happy. This will communicate to them that they have met your expectations and give them a dose of much-needed attention. Little People thrive on attention. While positive attention is preferable, be aware that even negative attention trumps no attention at all.

> I was having a conversation with a man the other day who didn't have children. Once he learnt what I do for a living he, like many others, gave me his two cents on modern day parenting. He mentioned how he finds it frustrating that children these days are 'over-praised' and are constantly told that they are doing 'good walking', 'good eating' and why not just say 'good breathing'. He was also bothered by the Little People on public trains who are chatted to constantly, never allowed to sit and form their own ideas about what they see out the window. He believed these chattering parents were almost trying to show off and prove to the rest of the carriage how good a parent they are.
>
> I stood and quietly listened to his side of the story before quietly asking 'Have you ever been in charge of a two year old on a train?'

WHAT IS ENCOURAGEMENT?

To encourage a child is to take notice of what they are doing that you would like to see more of. It is everything from the pre-planned sticker chart to the comment, 'Wow, you are doing great eating today!' This comment, by the way, is most effective two mouthfuls into dinner, before the battle begins. An encouraging environment is one where a child receives positive reinforcement for their positive behaviour.

Why is an encouraging environment important?

Encouragement promotes happy and confident Little People. Like the new employee who knows exactly what is expected of him/her, they will know what you want and how they can please you. They might even do more than you asked. Without being noticed and appreciated however, people (both Little and Big), will often feel disappointed, invisible and frustrated. Children live in a world where many things are unknown, they have strong impulses that are often inappropriate and they need help to know what to do, and that they are doing it right.

How can you use encouragement to keep your Little Person on track?

Encouragement is the positive reinforcement that balances your discipline. Try to set *expectations* and *boundaries* for your children even when it seems obvious what is expected of them. Say things like, 'When we get to the supermarket, I need you to use your inside voice and stay right next to me please'.

The next stage is to talk your Little Person through the scenario. Now that the expectations have been spelt out, you have the opportunity to talk to your child about how they are getting along. If they are doing as you asked, tell them! Maybe even get them an unexpected prize. Make a big deal about how awesome they are and how happy their behaviour is making you.

An added bonus is that you can calmly remind your Little Person when they get loud, 'Do you think that is an inside voice? Can you turn your volume down again please?' instead of growling 'Be quiet!'

Here are some ways to encourage your Little Person.

- As much as possible, ignore bad behaviour and find something positive to acknowledge instead.

- Distract a child that isn't doing what you want. Praise them ASAP once they change their actions.
- When you find yourself calm and enjoying your Little Person, tell them.
- Say things like: 'You're a star, I like the way you ...' 'Wow that was cool. It makes me happy when you ....'
- Start a Star Chart for the things your Little Person finds difficult. You could have things like good listening, finishing dinner and using kind words as behaviour that earns a reward.

The other 'E' in environment: Engagement

Little People are inquisitive and actively explore their world. Keeping Little People engaged is how you keep them from creating their own entertainment and getting into strife. Little People need to have their developing brains engaged in *something* all the time. So if you, as the Big Person provide activities, challenges, conversations and games, there is less time for your Little Person to create mischief.

. WHAT IS ENGAGEMENT?

It means to have your Little Person busy or occupied. It is when Little People are inspired, interested and inquisitive. Engaged children will show curiosity and attention. For the purpose of this chapter, we are talking about how we, as Big People, can keep our Little People engaged. Because we all know that Little People are very good at keeping themselves engaged, but usually they find fun in activities we'd rather they didn't! Some people argue that if we keep our littlies constantly engaged, they don't get to use their imagination. I say to them that imaginative play *is* engaging.

WHY IS ENGAGEMENT IMPORTANT?

Engaged children are happy children. They are learning, getting attention, developing new skills, practising old skills, and burning energy – mental and physical. They are learning focus and how to stay on task, determination, how to use their imagination, problem solve, entertain themselves in a socially acceptable way, easing boredom, becoming determined and learning how to connect with others.

Children are programmed to explore, experience and discover the world through engaging with it. They aren't made to sit and think, they are designed to *do*! They will naturally seek out experiences that develop their skills, challenge their abilities, test limits and answer questions. This is how they grow up. As my friend Sara explains it, 'If you run one kilometre every day for the rest of your life, you will never be able to run two kilometres. You have to push yourself outside of your comfort zone to grow and develop'.

And growing and developing is the name of the game for Little People. If we, as the Big People, can provide a fun and engaging environment for our children then we can enhance their learning and development. We can help them to push through to the second kilometre. They can't do this for themselves. They can't research a craft activity that they would like to do on Pinterest, or pop down to the shops or cut in a straight line. But you can! Doing this will help to direct their behaviour in a positive way. You can point them in the right direction to explore, experience and discover. This way they will learn socially acceptable ways to challenge themselves and your relationship won't get strained.

How can you keep your Little Person engaged?

- The easiest way is to just talk with them
- Play games
- Create activities
- Make things together
- Get them to help you with things like cooking, wrapping gifts and cleaning
- Sing

There are plenty of ideas in the chapter 'Constant engagement' in part three, and on my website. *www.angelicmonsters.com.au/engagement*

Action list:

- *Set expectations and boundaries for your children even when it seems obvious what is expected of them*
- *Say things like, 'When we get to the supermarket, I need you to use your inside voice and stay right next to me please'*
- *If they are doing as you asked, tell them they're awesome!*

- As much as possible, ignore bad behaviour and find something positive to acknowledge instead
- Distract a child that isn't doing what you want. Praise them ASAP once they change their actions
- Provide a fun and engaging environment
- Keep Little People inspired, interested and inquisitive

13. F IS FOR FOLLOW THROUGH

I meant what I said and I said what I meant

• Dr Seuss

If you say you're going to do a thing, do it. Follow through is about commitment to taking action. And if you aren't going to do it, don't say it. Little People are constantly testing the world and collecting data. They are learning machines. Sometimes you will be responsible for the reaction to their action. To make sure your words have meaning to Little People, you *must* do what you say you are going to. If you don't you will find yourself nagging and your Little Person will just ignore you and your idle threats. They have learned not to believe your words.

Following through isn't just about threats. You need to follow through on the positive things you say too. This will build trust and give your words power.

So what does it mean to follow through?

To follow through means to do as you say you're going to do and be careful not to say something if you don't intend to do it. A great example I see a lot is at the park when a frustrated Big Person will say to a Little Person, 'Don't do that or we will have to go home'. More often than not the Little Person will do that thing again and the Big Person will not take them home. That's a classic example of not following through.

A better thing to say at the park would be, 'If you do that again you're going to need to sit in the stroller'. It's a much easier thing to follow through with and it means that Big People don't have to miss out on the park just because Little People aren't being good listeners.

Why is following through important?

Following through is important because it teaches your Little Person they can trust you. It teaches them to take your words as truth and believe you when you say something. If you follow through consistently that means that when you threaten something (most of the time) just your words will be enough. Your Little Person will ignore you if they know you won't follow through. But if they believe that you mean what you say, they can make choices and know for sure what will happen.

How can you follow through?

If you find this one difficult, don't worry, you're not alone. Start with things that are easy to follow through with.

Think before you speak and only say something if you know you *really* mean it.

Have fun consequences sometimes. Say things like, 'If you go in the kitchen I'm gonna tickle you', then of course, do it.

Action list:

- *Think before you speak and only say something if you know you really mean it*
- *If you say you're going to do a thing, do it*
- *If you aren't going to do it, don't say it*

14. G IS FOR GRATITUDE

Gratitude is so important that we need to revisit it in a slightly different light. That is because I find it such a powerful tool for changing mindset. Not just yours, but your Little Person's too. By now you have been practising gratitude and keeping a journal of the things you are grateful for. Hopefully, you have started to notice the difference in the way you look at the world, the things you notice and how you now seek out things to appreciate. And you can share this powerful skill with your Little Person.

WHAT IS GRATITUDE?

Gratitude is an expression of thanks and appreciation. It is also an emotion. Generally the feeling lasts for only a few seconds, as a recognition of the actions of others that we really appreciate. Gratitude is a skill,

---

which can be learned. With practice and the right perspective, there will always be lots of things to be grateful for. Gratitude is one of the most effective methods for increasing long-term life satisfaction.

WHY IS IT IMPORTANT TO PRACTISE GRATITUDE?

Let me say that again: Gratitude is one of the most effective methods for increasing long-term life satisfaction.

Gratitude teaches us to acknowledge the positive experiences we have. You, as a Big Person, can use gratitude as a tool to get out of the habit of noticing your children's negative behaviour. If you are prone to nagging and losing your temper, this may be a useful tool for you.

Gratitude blocks negative emotions and helps both Big and Little People to be more stress resistant. It helps us to develop a higher sense of self-worth.

Gratitude will help you all to celebrate the present and stay in the moment. Little People are generally better at this that we are, so let *them teach you* this one.

One day I was taking a three year old boy, Luke, for a ride on the train, over the Sydney Harbour Bridge. Luke's grandfather decided that he wanted to hang out with us that day and when he asked what we were doing he was confused. 'Where are you going on the train?' I explained that the destination was the train. We were going into the city, but we would probably just come back straightaway. Poor Pa wasn't very pleased. He hated public transport, drove everywhere and couldn't understand why on earth we would take a train for fun. But he came with us anyway.

As we set off on our adventure, I watched Pa begin to light up. 'Look Luke! Here comes the train, toot, tooooot!' As we crossed the bridge Pa chatted to Luke about what he could see, excited by all the boats, the Opera House, the giant cruise liner going right beneath us. I will never forget the transformation of a jaded old man who hated public transport, suddenly seeing the world through three-year-old eyes. Everything was amazing, and exciting. Things he had seen literally hundreds of times before, were new again. This sense of rapture and wonder is one of my favourite things about spending my days with Little People. I think we are so lucky to be reminded by our Little People how awesome the world is. And not just 'awesome' in the casual, flippant sense that we use the word these days. I mean literally, in *awe*.

This appreciation for things that we normally wouldn't notice and really noticing the present moment, cultivates a sense of gratitude.

HOW CAN YOU HELP YOUR LITTLE PERSON TO PRACTISE GRATITUDE?

If they are old enough, help them to start their own gratitude diary. Remind them to write in it daily. Maybe you could do it together.

- At the dinner table, instead of the standard, 'How was your day, what did you learn at school?' ask, 'What are you grateful for today?' Make it a ritual to work gratitude into the conversation.
- Give kids chores. Sometimes getting Little People to do stuff is much harder than just doing it yourself, but it teaches them just how much effort goes into things. How can they be grateful if they have no idea what it takes to make a meal, set the table, clear up and do the dishes?
- Practise saying No. Parents who say Yes to their children lots often notice that instead of having happy children who are so pleased with all their cool stuff, they actually end up with greedy little consumers who never have quite enough. Saying no, and reminding them of that toy you bought last week is actually a more valuable lesson. All the Nos will make saying Yes so much more rewarding for both of you.
- Sponsor a child or donate to a charity. Educate your child about how lucky they are and help them to share with those in need. Talk to them about donating toys and clothes to charity as they grow out of them.
- Have your Little Person write Thank You notes to people who give them gifts and treats.

Action list:

- *Ask, 'What are you grateful for today?*
- *Perhaps start a journal. (What an awesome keepsake!)*
- *Give Little People chores*
- *Sponsor a child or donate to a charity. You could donate old clothes and toys to someone in need*

- *Have your Little Person write Thank You notes to people who give them gifts and treats*
- *Practise saying No*

Part III:
Top Secret Techniques

Here we are! The part you have been itching to get to. Now that you have spent the time making sure that you really *are* the Big Person your Little Person needs, and nailed the seven ABCs, you are ready to start on the big stuff!

First up, let's talk about some of the basic ideas you can use day to day for all types of battles. The beauty of these techniques is they stop most arguments before they even begin - prevention is better than cure. They will stop all the yelling, nagging and exasperation for you and help your Little Person to know exactly what is expected of them. It will help them to know when they are winning and when they are out of bounds.

Then we will move onto some more specific scenarios. These are the issues I see most often with the families I work with.

Imagine you are sitting down to watch some trashy TV (guilty pleasure – *The Bachelor*, right?). You hit the power button on your remote and nothing happens. What is the first thing you do? You push it harder. Maybe the button didn't notice that you pushed it. It might just need a good squeeze. So after you have pressed it so hard that you have a little dent in your thumb, you finally decide that the batteries are dead and you are going to have to try something else. You could either turn it on at the TV, or you could change the batteries.

This is exactly what will happen when you change your response to a behaviour that used to work for your Little Person. They will push that button harder and you need to be prepared for that. Wait patiently, as it *will pass* and they will eventually realise the 'batteries are dead' and they will try something else. Remember the first time is the longest and it will never be this hard again. Unless you give in … So be consistent and *follow through*!

15. Positive Reinforcement

Children live in a world of experimentation. They are constantly testing new behaviour and collecting data on the results they get. As Big People, the most effective way to have an impact on how our Little People choose to behave, is to *tell them what they are doing right*. We often find ourselves saying No, Don't and Stop *over and over again*. When this happens, try ignoring unwanted behaviour (more on this in the following chapters) and make an extra effort to tell Little People what you *do* want. And don't forget to make a big deal when they get it right. This simple technique is known as positive reinforcement and is a *total game changer*.

AVOID ACCIDENTAL POSITIVE REINFORCEMENT

Sometimes Big People accidentally positively reinforce negative behaviour. This reinforcement often happens in the form of attention. Attention can be very rewarding, even if it's negative attention.

So a Little Person who is interrupting his dad receives reinforcement every time his dad says, 'Stop that!' or 'Be quiet I'm talking.' Ignoring is the best way to respond to annoying attention-seeking behaviour.

Another way that Big People sometimes unintentionally reinforce negative behaviour is when they give in. If a parent tells a Little Person they can't watch TV, but then the child argues and cries until the Big Person gives in; the child's negative behaviour has been positively reinforced. The Little Person has learnt that whining helps them to get what they want and they are now likely to whine again in the future. So remember, always follow through.

Here are some great ways to get more positive reinforcement happening in your house:

Look for behaviour you like and comment on it

Sometimes it is just that simple. Tell your kids every time they are being awesome. They need to hear it. Yes, there is such a thing as over-praising, but especially with really Little People, praising positive behaviour is how they learn to direct behaviour in a positive way. If you're worried about 'over-praising' then only comment on new or developing behaviour. Skip the 'good drinking, walking and breathing' with 4 year olds. They should have nailed those skills.

Start a star chart

1. Choose 3-5 behaviours you would like to see more of in your Little Person. Write them up on a chart. Include pictures if you can, to help your Little Person 'read' the chart. Also make them positive. So instead of saying 'no fighting,' write 'being kind' instead. Ignoring = good listening. Refusing dinner = great eating.
2. Talk to your Little Person and explain your new chart. Make sure they are very clear on the behaviours that you are looking for.
3. Quickly start rewarding small examples of the positive behaviour.

It is important to give lots of stickers quite freely at the beginning of the process. If you are a stingy sticker giver, the chart will flop because your Little Person will feel like the stickers are unachievable. Aim to fill an entire chart in the first week of using one, then make another.

4. Give a massive dose of positive attention when you put stickers up. The 'Woo hoo' from you is what gives the stickers their value. Call Grandma, proudly tell the other kids at the park, just make a big deal!

5. Try to give stickers straightaway when you notice the behaviour you are looking for.

6. For Little People that are under 4 or new to this, usually just the stickers will be enough to make their little chests puff out. Sometimes however, it's useful to have something they are working towards. Maybe twenty stickers will earn them an experience they have been hanging out for. A trip to the skate park, the zoo or to see a movie. You can also use material rewards like food treats and toys, but I tend to shy away from these.

There is a chart you could download for free from my website: www.angelicmonsters.com.au/charts

Action list:

- *Make an extra effort to tell Little People what you do want*
- *Avoid accidental positive reinforcement*
- *Be aware of what you pay attention to*
- *Look for behaviour you like and comment on it*
- *Start a star chart. Find a free one online at www.angelicmonsters.com.au/charts*

16. Constant Engagement

Idle hands are the devil's playthings
• proverb (and my Grandpa)

What is the best way to keep Little People out of trouble?

Keep them busy with things that you want them to do. Constantly. Don't worry, this is actually much easier than it sounds.

Little People need to have their developing brains engaged in something all the time. You can give them something to do to keep them engaged or they will create their own entertainment, and while that can be absolutely gorgeous, it can lead to disaster. Noisy, messy, disaster that is out of your control.

So what can we do to keep Little People engaged? This is something that you will be asking yourself for a few years, and you will find things that work like magic for your Little Person and things that don't. I have compiled a list of thought starters, and I really encourage you to use your imagination, follow your toddler's lead and don't be embarrassed by what others will think of you while you play with your children. (Many Big People say they feel silly playing with their children in public). Who is more important? Besides, people probably aren't thinking the nasty things you think they are anyway! (Remember- they are thinking about their breakfast!)

In a café:

- Pull out a bunch of those little sugars and make shapes with them. Show your Little Person how to make a triangle, house, six-pointed star and get them to copy you.
- Crayons are your best friend, and keep a supply of paper or cardboard in your car.

In the supermarket:

- Let your Little Person loose with a mission, 'Can you help me to get three bananas, one orange and a bread stick?'
- Get them to count the lights while sitting in the trolley. This has the added bonus of having their eyes averted from all the colourful, tasty, argument-starting treats.

In the car:

- Play 'I spy with my little eye something beginning with ...' If your child doesn't know the alphabet then you could use colours.
- Another great alphabet game is the Name Game. You choose a category, say animals, objects, boys' or girls' names and then take turns to think of something starting with each letter. For example: Animals. Anteater, bear, cat, dog, elephant, and so on.
- Rhyming words. Can you think of something that rhymes with the word 'star'?
- Name that tune. Hum a song and get your Little Person to guess what song it is.

Where there is space to run around:

- My all-time favourite is a game my cousin Emma made up. It's called *Run Like a Cheetah*. First you establish a boundary so children know how far to run, then get them to run 'like a cheetah' to that place and come back like a ... Get your Little Person swaying like elephants, flapping like birds, wriggling like worms and hopping like kangaroos. If you run out of ideas then get them to use their acting skills to be an animal and you can guess which one they are. Keep going until they are worn out. Which doesn't take long at all! The best bit? You don't even have to move.
- Play 'tips'. Chase each other around like crazy people. It's great exercise for everyone!
- Hide and seek.

Here are some more ways to keep your Little Person engaged.

CRAFT

Craft is a fantastic way to develop your Little Person's creativity, fine motor skills and attention span. Making things is fun and easy and will delight your Little Person. Remember that the process, rather than the finished product is what is valuable to Little People. You might see a whole page coloured in with just one colour. They see their ability to manipulate objects and transform white paper into red.

If you haven't made anything before and think you are no good at craft, don't despair. Start with one of these simple activities:

- Tear up some coloured paper with your Little Person. Then cover a whole page in glue and help them to stick all the bits on. You could do this with pictures cut out of magazines, or printed off the interwebs. Little People love to Google images and choose a few to print! Collage is easy and looks great.
- Paint some hand and footprints. Have the wipes ready if you're worried about mess. If you're not so worried, why not set up outside. Get a big piece of butcher's paper, strip your Little Person down to their nappy, plonk them in the middle and give them some paint and brushes. This is great fun so remember to have your camera ready! I often frame the picture of the paint-covered baby along

with a piece of the art they were creating. (Note: When buying paint always check that it is non-toxic and washable).

- If you really, really don't like mess then put some blobs of paint on a piece of paper and then slide it into a big zip lock bag. Let your Little Person mix the paint around while you smile about how clean everything is.
- Chalk drawing. Need I say more? Buy some jumbo chalk, a patch of concrete/wall/bricks/pavement and get down and dusty with your Little Person.

PLAY

Children learn through play. They use play to express themselves even before they have the words to explain how they feel. It allows children to be in charge and build confidence in themselves. Play is a place where children can be in control, which is a rare thing in this world that is organised by adults. Little People play for fun. They can play what they enjoy and stop when they want to. Remember this when playing with your Little Person. If it isn't fun, something isn't right.

While playing, children learn how to:

- Give and take in relationships with their friends
- Lead and follow
- Think about what they want to do and to plan
- Use their imagination and creativity
- Create their own fun and de-stress
- Mend mistakes
- Enjoy magical worlds!

Some ideas of games to play with your Little Person:

- Card games. These will change depending on how old your Little Person is. A game of memory with 2-20 pairs of cards. Go fish. Snap. Uno. Maybe even a simple version of Rummy.
- Play basketball with soft toys and a big bucket. From how far away can you get the toys in? You could also use scrunched up paper and a wastebasket.
- Get out some musical instruments or pots and pans and have a jam session.

- Choose 3-10 objects and have a treasure hunt. Take turns hiding the objects and finding them again.
- Imagine you are animals and play 'family'.
- Set up a bunch of cushions and play Leapfrog from one to the other.
- Visit Angelic Monsters online for many more ideas!

If you are looking for activities to do with your children, check out my website: www.angelicmonsters.com.au/engagement

Action list:

- *Think of the places you are most likely to get into a battle with your Little Person. The cafe, supermarket and doctors' waiting room are all goldmines. Think of some games and activities that you can have up your sleeve for next time you are there*
- *Always be prepared. The Uno cards live in my handbag. Sometimes Big People like to play while they wait too!*
- *Find ways to use your environment to challenge Little People. How many times can you _____, how fast can you _____, can you count _____*
- *You can always talk about colours, numbers, letters and shapes*
- *Bring a book – or three*
- *Exercise is a great way to keep Little People engaged*

17. Magic Questions

These questions have the ability to revolutionise your relationship with your Little Person. Yes and No questions often get the answer you *don't* want to hear. (Think: Do you want to wear a hat?) Straight out directions aren't always useful. They can trigger major power battles. They make Big People out to be a dictator and Little People feel frustrated, belittled and defiant.

So how can you get your Little Person doing what you want them to, without dictating, lecturing and nagging? *Ask questions and give directions in an OR format.*

Or questions are magic because you can give Little People the control that they desire, without giving it away totally. Do not underestimate the magic of this Ninja power!

This is how it's done:

'Timmy, put your shoes on.'

'No.'

'Timmy, I told you to put your shoes on. Do it now please.'

'No.' (I could keep going forever, but you see where I'm taking this, right?)

Here is the magic of an Or question.

'Timmy, would you like to wear your red shoes, or your blue ones?'

'Ummm, my red ones! They go faster ...'

'Great, would you like to put them on yourself or shall I help you?'

'I want to do it.'

'Great, while you do that I'm going to pack your lunch. What would you like on your sandwich? Vegemite or ham and cheese?'

Life seems a little simpler in this scenario, doesn't it? The uses for this trick are endless. Here are some ideas for you:

- Would you like to go to the park or the beach?
- Where are you going to sit? In your highchair or at the Big People's table?
- Are you going to wear your hat or just carry it?
- Should we play cars or dominoes first?
- Would you like to have a bath now or in 5 minutes?
- Peas or carrots today?

  Or if the carrots aren't optional: Would you like two or three carrot sticks?
- While the magic of Or questions is life-changing, there are a few traps you should look out for:
- Make sure both are options that make you happy so it doesn't matter which they choose.
- If your child is prone to the dreaded 'Ummmmmmmmmmmmmmmmmmmmmmmmmmm', give them about 10 seconds and then make the choice for them. Before they can protest, offer them another choice to distract them.

Using the example from earlier, say you asked Timmy if he would like to wear his red shoes or his blue ones and he said, 'Neither', don't let this rattle you. You have two options. You can just choose for him and move onto the next Or question. 'Okay, well I choose your blue ones, they match your jacket. Are you going to put them on or shall I?' The other option is to give a different choice altogether. 'Well, you need shoes to go to the park. Would you like to put your shoes on and go out, or we can stay inside with bare feet. You choose.'

Another bonus of the OR question is that when it comes time to give a direction that isn't presented as a choice children will be less inclined to battle. If you give a direction like, 'Time for bed, off we go!' and your Little Person protests, you can say something like, 'Remember all the choices that you made today? Now it's my turn, thank you'. You will find that there will be less 'digging in of heels'.

Action list:

- *When giving your Little Person a direction, present it as an OR question*
- *Only offer two options, both of which will please you*
- *If your Little Person takes more than 10 seconds to choose, choose for them and quickly distract them with the next choice*

18. Give One Warning then Do as You Promise!

This concept of *give one warning* is perfectly executed with a sentence that I use all of the time:

If you do this <good thing>, then I will do this <good thing>. But if you do that <bad thing>, then I will do that <bad thing>. You choose...

This is my favourite sentence to use with Little People. It does three things. It outlines a positive action and reward, a negative action and a consequence, and gives the Little Person the power to choose their own adventure. All the Big Person needs to do is follow through on what they have promised. The concept of *following through* is so important, that's why an entire chapter was dedicated to it earlier.

It is important to give a warning before disciplining your child. Just one is enough or you will turn into a broken record. The only time you should swoop without all the pre-emptive chit-chat is when a child's safety is at risk – like when they run into the road or when they become violent.

Here are some examples of how you could use the *You choose* sentence. And remember to make the reward/consequences *relevant*.

Before:	After:
Get ready, we are leaving.	If you get dressed, we can go to the park. But if you stay in your pyjamas we have to stay here, and you will miss out on seeing your friends. You choose.
Eat your dinner.	If you eat all the food on your plate and you are still hungry, you can have dessert. If you don't eat your dinner you can't have anything else. You choose.
Get in the bath.	If you hop in the bath now then we will have time to play afterwards but if you muck about then it will be bedtime by the time we are done. You choose.
Stay in your chair at the table.	If you use your beautiful table manners, you can stay at the table with us. But if you keep getting up, you will have to sit in your highchair like a baby. You choose.
Stop fighting!	If you play nicely together I'll get the Lego out, but if you squabble, you can play separately in your rooms. You choose.

Action list:

- Outline your expectations for your Little Person as often as you can
- Practise, practise, practise!
  Post this up on your wall: (there is a pretty version online at www.angelicmonsters.com.au/charts

If you If you do this :)
Then I will do this: :)
But if you do that: :(
Then I will do that: :(
You choose...

19. Negative Reinforcement

1..2..3..

The biggest problem with modern day parenting is
positive reinforcement for negative behaviour
• a bikie/school teacher I met in a pub in New Zealand.

This chapter covers the ways you can use attention removal as a negative consequence for negative behaviour. This involves ignoring, distracting and walking away from Little People. Sometimes these techniques aren't enough. If you need bigger consequences, hold tight, they are in the next chapter.

Keep in mind the 'power button on the remote' story at the beginning of part two (page 90). This is where it is most relevant. Your Little

Person is used to getting a certain response when they do things. Now that you will begin ignoring those things, your Little Person will push harder before they realise there is a better way to get what they need. Be prepared to ride out the initial stage. It will get better, and the more you practise; the quicker it happens.

We really need to be careful what we reward in our children's behaviour. When they are doing things that we don't like, we need to offer a negative response. One way we can do this is to offer no attention as a consequence. *Completely ignoring a child* sends a very loud message to them. It may seem simple. In the moment it can seem impossible. But especially with really Little People, ignoring is your best friend. Seriously.

How can you use attention removal to help train your Little Person to become a functioning adult in our society?

If they are doing something you don't like ... just ignore it! Don't pay attention to it or give any response whatsoever because attention is what your children are trying to achieve. *Any* attention, be it positive or negative is actually *rewarding* that behaviour. So the most powerful tool is to turn a blind eye and pretend it's not happening. Go and do something else. Your brain should sound like this:

'Sorry what's that? You're having a tantrum? Oh wow, suddenly something in the kitchen is just calling my name.' When you do this properly, children will stop behaving that way because they are not getting the reaction they want. Whatever you pay attention to will keep happening, so you just have to choose what will work to get you engaged and what won't.

The flip-side of this technique is that you really need to be ready with your positive reinforcement skills. So when you are on the phone and they are yelling 'Mummy! Mummy! Mummy! Mummy! Muuuuuuuuuuuuuummmmmmmmmmmmmmmmm!' and you decide to ignore it, firstly, explain to the person on the phone what you are doing and be really involved in that conversation as you turn your back and walk into another room. Secondly, *as soon as your Little Person stops yelling* at you and waits patiently for you to be finished, you *must* recognise and praise this behaviour – *instantly*. This *positive reinforcement for positive behaviour* is the key element to modifying behaviour using attention removal.

When using this technique give yourself something to do. So you're not paying attention to the fact that you aren't paying attention. Children will sense if you are just pretending to not pay attention. You need to actually be engaged in something else.

Some things you can do while you are waiting for your Little Person to change their behaviour:

- Walk into another room
- Read a book
- Have a snack
- Do something you enjoy

ATTENTION REMOVAL STEP-BY-STEP

Your child is doing something that is outside your boundaries of what is acceptable. What should you do?

For the little things:

1. Notice the behaviour.
2. Decide if it is appropriate to ignore this behaviour. Is it safe?
3. Begin ignoring. Don't talk to or make eye contact with your child.
4. Really ignore them don't just pretend. Little People know when you are faking it so leave the room, do the dishes, grab a book, whatever works for you. A brilliant option is to grab one of the kids' toys and start playing with it, usually a Little Person will stop what they are doing and come and join in! More on this below in the art of distraction.
5. Follow through. Don't ignore behaviour for 2 minutes, then change tactics and swoop in for a lecture. It's got to be like water off a duck's back.
6. When the child ceases the behaviour or tries something nice to get your attention, tune back in and reward the new positive behaviour.
7. Move on.
8. Later, when you are both in a good headspace, talk about what they were doing, why you ignored them and what they could do instead in the future.

The art of distraction

Notice the behaviour.

Decide if distraction is appropriate.

Use the tools you have available to come up with something to ask/talk about/do that will distract your child from whatever they are doing.

Move on.

Later, when you are both in a good headspace, talk about what they were doing, why you ignored them and what they could do instead in the future.

Some examples:

- As you walk past the cafe, 'I want a cookie!', 'Can you see that plane? Look up there! What colour is it?'
- Your child tries to snatch another child's toy at the park. 'Hey look, there are some swings, let's see how high you can go today!' (Important sidenote: this isn't a question. If you said, 'Do you want to go on the swing?' the answer would be, 'No, I want to play with that toy'.)
- Your Little People are fighting, so you turn your back, find a game they love and start playing with it. 'Oh wow, this game is so great! Look what I found!'

Walking away

1. Notice the behaviour.
2. Decide if it is appropriate to walk away. Is it safe? This strategy works best with temper tantrums.
3. If you aren't sure it is safe to leave them, turn your back and ignore their tantrum.
4. *Never let the tantrum work.* It will exponentially increase the chances of tantrums happening again (and again ... and again ...)
5. Walk away.
6. Be patient.
7. Comfort your child when they come to you, but don't give them what they were tantrumming for.
8. Move on.

Later, when you are both in a good headspace, talk about what they were doing, why you ignored them and what they could do instead in the future.

How to Be the Big Person Your Little Person Needs

For bigger stuff

See the next chapter 'Final straw'.

Action list:

- When your Little Person is behaving in an unacceptable manner, ignore them
- Do something else. Children can spot a faker from a mile off. Really ignore them, don't just pretend
- Wait for your child to try a new, more appropriate way to get what they want
- When they are being awesome, pay lots of attention – instantly

20. 'FINAL STRAW'

When a child has tested and found a boundary enough times to know that they are crossing it, sometimes Big People need a 'final straw' to send a clear message that this behaviour will not be tolerated.

This chapter outlines some discipline techniques when ignoring, distraction and walking away aren't working.

TIME-OUT

Give *one* warning. If you keep _____, you will need to go to time-out, but if you _____ instead, we can _____. For example: 'If you keep hitting your sister, you will need to go to time-out, but if you are gentle instead, we can build a pillow fort together.'

If the behaviour continues, swiftly start the time-out process as follows:

1. Put the child in the time-out place, maybe a specific chair, step or place on the floor.
2. Get down to their level and explain why they are there.
3. Leave the child for 1 minute for each year of their age. For example, 4 years = 4 minutes.
4. Ignore everything that the child does, until they have sat quietly for their time. If they leave the time-out spot, firmly say, 'No, you must stay on the step/chair for ___ minutes' as you put them back the *first time only*. After that, just put them back. (This could go on for a while if your Little Person is used to being in charge. Just be consistent, follow through and it will pass.
5. When the minutes are over, go and get down to the Little Person's level again and ask them, 'Do you know why you are on time-out? Why is that not okay? How would you feel if someone did that to you?'
6. Get them to say *Sorry* to whoever is appropriate.
7. Give them a big kiss and a cuddle.
8. Move on.

Getting down to their level means bringing your eyes to their level. Standing over children and looking down on them can be very dominating and make your child feel small and powerless.

Getting down on your knees and talking to them will make you more vulnerable, less scary and make them much more likely to understand what you are trying to communicate.

When disciplining children, talk about feelings. They will feel validated and less defiant or frustrated.

Here are some ways to do this:

- When you hit me it makes me feel sad.
- I know wearing your helmet is frustrating but it keeps you safe.
- How would you feel if someone did that to you?

How to Be the Big Person Your Little Person Needs

Don't lose your marbles!

This is a barter system to use with your Little Person. The marbles represent something; usually time-based, like 30 minutes of screen time or one-on-one time before bed. So in this scenario each marble is worth 5 minutes. Children lose marbles throughout the day for inappropriate behaviour, and the thing I like best about this system is that they can *earn their marbles back*. So even if everyone has had a challenging day and your Little Person has no marbles left, you could ask them to do some jobs to earn a couple back. (That way you get a few minutes of downtime too!) I have seen this technique absolutely transform households. Simple but very effective as the value of the marbles can change as your children grow. It might even become a percentage of pocket money later. The visual representation helps your Little Person to see their percentage, which otherwise they wouldn't understand.

1. Get 6 marbles for each Little Person and put them in a glass.
2. Decide what each marble is worth for the child. 5 minutes/10 minutes? Screen time? Quiet one-on-one time before bed? Make it something your child really values. If they watch lots of TV, that half hour won't matter to them so choose something else.
3. Explain to the whole family the new system.
4. When a Little Person is acting out warn them *once* that if they continue, they will lose a marble.
5. If they continue, take one marble away and explain that they have just lost some of their special time for the day.
6. When special time comes work out how much time they have and set a timer.

If they have lost marbles, make a point when the time is up: 'What a shame you can't see what happens at the end of the show, maybe tomorrow you'll keep all your marbles'. You need to make the marbles valuable!

Often people ask, 'What if I have two children and they have a different number of marbles at the end of the day?' This is actually very useful. If one sibling is getting extra time for being better behaved, that is really going to motivate them both to keep from losing their marbles the next day!

'Get back in your bed, now!' Gina yelled at her son for the umpteenth time. He stood at the top of the stairs looking down at her at the bottom. Frustrated and in a rage, he picked up a candle, one of those heavy ones set in glass. He threw it at her.

This happened just before this family called me. Things had gotten out of hand and Gina was frightened of her 6-year-old son. He had been getting more defiant for a while now and what started as school refusal had now grown into a violent lashing out. Gina's son wouldn't listen to instructions, he was misbehaving regularly and whenever his Big People needed him to do something, he would make it a battle. Time-out was useless because getting him to stay where he was supposed to was not worth the fight.

So what did I do? I went back to the ABCs of course! Missing in this household was clear discipline, follow through and the environment lacked encouragement and positive reinforcement. I called a family meeting where everyone had a safe space to talk about how they felt and what they thought about what was happening. I introduced the family to my marble system where the boys would lose 5 minutes of screen time if they didn't behave and started a family reward chart. This chart was really special as each family member (even mum and dad) got to choose three skills they thought they could work on, and once they had gained 20 stars, they earned a reward. Everyone in the family chose a personal 'experience' reward, and they worked together to come up with a big group activity they could do when everyone had completed their chart. The boys chose a trip to Luna Park and horse riding, while mum chose a facial and dad a day of golf. Once everyone had completed the challenge, there was a family trip to the local waterpark to be had! The change in behaviour was amazing. Praising the boys for doing the right thing boosted their confidence and made them eager to do the right thing for attention. The marbles provided a clear consequence for bad behaviour and one warning usually proved to be enough to change their behaviour.

If you think this idea might work for you too, there is a free printable chart on my website: *www.angelicmonsters.com.au/charts*

Time-In

If your Little Person gets a bit over-excited and tends to get in trouble a lot when this happens a great idea is *time-in*.

Instead of sending them away to time-out to calm down, use some time-in instead. This is where you set your child a task that they must complete before they are ready to rejoin the action. Maybe it is a puzzle or finding a picture of something specific in a big book or magazine.

1. Have a task that you know your child likes and can achieve on their own.
2. When things escalate, give your Little Person *one* warning. If they continue, they will need to spend some time-in.
3. If they continue, set them up with their task and explain what they need to do before they can rejoin you.
4. When they finish their task, talk to them about what they were doing that caused the time-in, why it was inappropriate and how they could do better next time.

Bedtime adjustments

1. Some Big People adjust their Little People's bedtimes as a consequence. Bedtime gets earlier by 5-minute increments. *Do not* use this technique if you have any issues with bedtime. It works best with children over 3 years of age.
2. When your Little Person plays up, give them *one* warning that if they continue you will move their bedtime forward by 5 minutes.
3. At bedtime, put your Little Person to bed at the time they have earned. For example, if their bedtime is usually 7, and you have had to use this technique twice, take them to bed at 10 minutes to 7.
4. Explain that it is bedtime early, remind them why this is happening and talk about what they could do instead in the future.

Job Jar

Having a jar full of chores is like having a Not-so-Lucky Dip as a consequence for improper behaviour. To use this technique you need to be sure that your children will do the chores without it being another battle. Only use this one if you know your Little People will do as they are told. Works best with children over 5 years of age.

1. Brainstorm a list of chores with your family.
2. Write each one on its own little piece of paper.
3. Put all your jobs in a big jar. If it looks a bit empty, come up with more jobs, or double up on the ones you have.
4. When a Little Person is misbehaving, give them one warning. 'If you continue, you will need to do a job from the job jar.'
5. If they continue, get them to dip their hand in the jar and randomly choose a job. No switching allowed!
6. Get them to do the job. If they dawdle, take away privileges until the task is completed.
7. When they finish their job, talk to them about what they were doing that caused the discipline, why it was inappropriate and how they could do better next time.

Action list:

- *Choose a strategy from the list above and discuss it with your partner*
- *If you both agree on a method and are 100% committed to following through, write the steps up and stick them up somewhere visible*
- *Practise doing all the steps properly*
- *Don't lose heart if it is a bit rocky at the beginning, change takes time*
- *Find support if you need help!*

21. SLEEP

As a parent, you are going to be a little bit obsessed with sleep. You won't get as much as you would like for a while, and sleep deprivation may nearly unstitch you. This will pass. There are things in the following chapters that will shorten this phase. If you haven't slept more than 90 minutes at a time for the last 2 years, read this bit twice. We are going to fix it! If you have a stunning baby that isn't old enough to sleep through the night yet, also read this bit twice. Prevention is better than any cure.

Going to sleep and eating are the two main things that your Little Person is in complete control of. In a battle of the wills, your toddler will have the final say on whether they swallow that bean or power down for the day and go to sleep.

This is okay, we just need to change the rules of the battle and make the swallowing and sleeping a product of our victory.

ROUTINES

Little People like to know what is coming next. They really don't like having things sprung on them. (Maybe this is because they are massive control freaks).

Routines are invaluable when it comes to raising Little People. After reading 'A routine' at the beginning of part two you should be following some form of routine, and that is a great place to start. This chapter covers bedtime routines. They will minimise the battles and make bedtime a breeze (most of the time).

One of the greatest gifts you can set up for yourself, is a solid bedtime routine. This is something you can start when your Little Person is brand new, or already terrorising your adult quiet time. It is so important that adults get to have some grown-up time after Little People go to bed. This time is for maintaining your relationship, having conversations without being interrupted, being able to switch off and relax, or for that sanity-saving glass of wine ... Actually, maybe it's not the wine that is saving your sanity, it's just having the space to drink it peacefully.

So, that solid bedtime routine. You want to be putting your Little Person down at the *same time each day*. There is something magical about getting kids to sleep at 7pm. It means that their sleep cycles will have them waking at about 5:30am, when it is still dark, then doing another 90 minute cycle. That means they wake at 7am the next morning. Woohoo! If they go to sleep at 7:30pm, they will reach a wake cycle at about 6am and if it's light, it's all over Red Rover.

Another important factor is having a series of relaxing events that you repeat right before bedtime every day. The whole routine should last half an hour or 45 minutes. This means that from the moment they get into the bath, their minds are gearing towards bedtime. Have you ever tried to go straight from work or the gym to bed? It's not ideal. Our minds need time to gear down.

Some popular activities are:

- Having a bath
- Brushing teeth
- Listening to calm music
- Reading some books together
- Talking quietly about your day
- Cuddling.

Find a set of activities that work for you, grab some felt-tipped pens and put them up on the wall so everyone at home knows the drill.

It is essential that at least for the first week you are really consistent with your routine, especially if you are already having troubles. Once your Little People know the ritual, it is possible to deviate a bit from the timetable, but beware: inconsistency from you will be mirrored by them. So try not to disrupt their idea of how the world works too often.

A few things that will get you into trouble down the track:

- Putting your baby to bed already asleep (more on that in the next chapter).
- Having things that assist your baby to get to sleep once in bed. Things like patting, feeding, music playing, cuddles in bed. Basically anything you don't intend to provide each time they wake throughout the night. Which is anywhere from once every 45 minutes to every 90 minutes (like us!).
- Not starting early enough. If bedtime is 7pm and you have a 45-minute routine then that means dinner has to be finished by 6:15pm. Plan for how long your child takes to eat, and have dinner ready before then.

Action list:

- Design your 'lead-up to bedtime' routine
- Have at least five relaxing activities to do every day before bed
- Write them out and stick them up!
- Be consistent

TEACHING TO SELF-SETTLE

People, both Big and Little, sleep in cycles. We all wake up somewhere between every 45 minutes to 90 minutes. If you don't really notice how often you wake up at night, you can thank your own Big Person for teaching you how to settle yourself to sleep with no assistance.

I'm about to share with you a very important piece of information. Probably one of the most important in this entire book. This is the trick to having Little People that sleep *all night*. To have our children wake up, turn themselves over and go back to sleep *without any help* is the only way you will have a Little Person that will sleep for 12 hours a night.

Every single family that I have worked with to fix night waking didn't know this. Or maybe they knew but didn't live by it. If your Little Person falls asleep with a breast/dummy/bottle in their mouth, they will wake up, wonder where it has gone, and ask for it to be brought back. This can be the same for many, many 'sleep crutches' all the way down to your very presence.

What does your Little Person need to go to sleep? The ideal answer is nothing. It is never too late to teach your Little Person to sleep unassisted.

The quickest way to change sleep habits is to go cold turkey on sleep assistance and do some form of controlled crying. If you aren't into that, that's okay, there are other options. Start with the 7pm bedtime and daytime naps using the following settling techniques, and never take backwards steps. Remember, it takes about *two weeks* of solid consistency to change behaviour, and only *one slip-up to send you back to square one*.

While being able to put themselves to sleep with no help is the ideal, I recognise that sometimes Little People need a bit of encouragement. These are some settling techniques that I have used 'in case of emergency' with sick or unfamiliar children. I also use these techniques to gradually step down the amount of sleep assistance a Little Person needs when first teaching a long-term waker to resettle themselves. The key to these techniques is that you step closer and closer to the final goal of having your Little Person settle *on their own*. Don't get trapped in the exponential amount of patting. If you find that you are needing to do more, not less for your Little Person, you aren't teaching them to sleep on their own at all.

THE BAD GUYS

Feeding

This is a common and especially unfair settling tool. Firstly, there is no milk dispenser in your Little Person's bed, so they have to fully wake up, scream to get your attention and wait for you to deliver their next sleeping dose. I would hate to have to do that every hour or so! The other thing that makes this so unfair for your child is that it is really not good for their health. Bottles in bed are bad for teeth and often cause other health issues like ear infections. (To avoid this, make sure you prop them up while they are feeding).

How to Be the Big Person Your Little Person Needs

Dummies

These magical plugs can be such a trap. I recommend that if you choose to use one to calm down your Little Person or stretch out their routine, don't let them fall asleep with one in their mouth. As they relax their jaw it will drop out and they will need you to help them find it to go back to sleep.

Co-sleeping

Dangerous for little babies and adults' sex lives, co-sleeping isn't ideal. While you don't have to get up and down while you are breastfeeding, be prepared to be up and down playing musical beds for many years to come if you choose this road. Co-sleeping is often a last resort at 3am after you have tried everything else. Beware that you are teaching your child that if they kick up a big enough fuss, for long enough, they will get to sleep in your bed.

Cuddling to sleep

Imagine you are in the arms of your lover. You are warm and comfortable and you happily doze off. After what feels like a second you open your eyes in a cold, dark room, flat on a mattress surrounded by bars.

This is how it feels for your Little Person. No doubt, they will cry when they wake and need you to come back and repeat the process again. Remember this is going to happen as often as every 45 minutes. Not fun for anyone really.

Going for a drive or a walk around the block

Are you prepared to do this every night for the next several years? This isn't teaching your Little Person to sleep by themselves. It's just a life-hack that babies fall asleep while moving. In the moment, great plan. Long term? Disaster.

THE LESS-BAD GUYS

Patting/rocking

A step down from the Bad Guys, patting or rocking your baby can be a useful tool for keeping little ones from freaking out. Staying with your Little Person until they are calmly dozing or fast asleep and giving them physical comfort can be a great help when you are teaching them to sleep in their own beds with no bottle, dummy, cuddling, or being in your bed. It is however a means to an end, and be careful that two minutes of gentle patting doesn't gradually turn into an hour.

Wrapping/swaddling

Wrapping really little babies is amazing. It stops them from startling themselves and makes them feel comforted (squashed!) like when they were in the womb. I always wrap newborns to sleep. Wrap them tight, think uterus-tight. Make sure their little legs can move though. When it's time to ditch the wrapping, leave first one arm, then both arms out before stopping the wrapping altogether.

Staying in the room

Sitting or lying in your Little Person's room as they go to sleep, *without giving them any attention*, can comfort them to know that you are still there, but it isn't playtime. If you are going to use this technique you must not engage with your child. Sit quietly in their room and read a book or something until they fall asleep. Depending on your child and what they are used to, they may put on a major performance. They might try absolutely every trick in the book to get you check back in. Just carry on minding your own business. Don't talk to them, make eye contact or acknowledge their carry-on in any way. If they are getting out of bed, calmly pick them up and plonk them back. This might seem fun for a little while, but if you really stay detached, it gets old pretty quickly. Just stick to your guns and follow through.

Using white noise and night lights

Sometimes white noise really helps Little People sleeping in noisy environments. And night lights are a great tool for children who are frightened of the dark, or need to visit the toilet in the night.

Leave them to work it out

Some babies happily go to sleep all on their own from day one.

Some babies just cry themselves to sleep. They will cry every time you put them into bed, and that's okay. They cry for a little while, then they go to sleep. Often Big People find this very distressing and will go in and try to settle the child and when they leave again, the baby will be more distressed. In my experience, the best thing to do with these Little People, is to just leave them go to sleep. The less you interrupt them, the faster they go to sleep. If you are anxious as your baby cries, a video monitor can help. Remember that consistency is key, so if you know that you can't listen to your baby cry, this isn't the method for you.

The chair method

The chair method is an alternative to leaving your Little Person alone. This method can be particularly challenging though, especially if your Little Person is older. Make sure you have someone to help you when it all gets a bit hard.

1. Talk about what is going to happen at bedtime, throughout the day, so your Little Person is aware.
2. Follow your five-step bedtime routine.
3. After you have said goodnight, turned out the lights etc., sit in a chair right by your Little Person's bed. Sit quietly and give them no attention. Don't talk, no eye contact. Just relax. Meditate.
4. If your Little Person gets up, lay them back down. The first time say, "It's time for bed now, show me how you can go to sleep." The second time say, "It's sleep time now" and after that say NOTHING. No eye contact. No attention for negative behaviour. The idea is to make it so boring, sleep is more fun.
5. As your Little Person gets comfortable with the process and goes to sleep with no drama, move your chair a few centimetres towards the door each day until you are sitting in the doorway.
6. Usually by the time you are in the door, the Little Person is quite used to you being far away but to make sure they know you are still there as you move the chair around the corner, make sure you

make some noises. Cough, turn pages loudly, hum a little, make a quiet phone call.

7. If this goes well and your Little Person goes to sleep without being able to see you, from here you can do your five-step bedtime routine, say goodnight, turn off the light and walk out. Then go and do something NOISY! Don't be silent. The banging and clanging of the dishes lets your Little Person know you are still there. It makes them feel safe.

I'll be back in five minutes

One thing I always do (whether I have used the chair method or not) is I say, "I'll come back in five minutes to see how you're going". Then I go back in five minutes. If the Little Person is still awake I give them another kiss goodnight and say the same thing. I do this every five minutes until they are asleep. You could also say, "I just have to go and do the dishes, then I'll come back". Or "I'm going to do a wee, I'll be back in one minute". These are a great way to start using this trick. This builds trust and lets them know that I am still there keeping them safe. It also gets a bit boring waiting for you and helps those eyelids get heavy.

Another thing I do, is in those five minute intervals I make *noise*. I bang and clang and do the dishes. I sweep and let the broom bang into things, scrape the chairs along the floor, collect the washing and hum to myself. I leave the volume up on the TV letting the hum of voices reach the kids' room. I let the kids know I am still there, and I'm doing boring stuff not worth getting out of bed to witness. I have noticed that families have a habit of shutting down all noise as their Little People go to sleep. Tiptoeing around, telling visitors to shhhh and leaving the noisy jobs until later. This can make your Little People wonder where you have gone and come out to check that you are still there. It may also make them very light sleepers in the future.

Some other things to consider:

- Make sure you know your Little Person's cues and put them down early enough. Over-tired Little People will find it very difficult to get to sleep.
- Many parents try adjusting nap-times. Usually more sleep in the day

is the answer. Sleep encourages sleep, though some people swear by dropping the naps. Experiment and keep a record.

- No screens just before bed, it keeps brains awake.
- For children that take a while to wind down have reading time or recorded meditations.
- Recognise that all children are different and what worked for your other children or someone else's child isn't necessarily going to be the answer for your Little Person.

Jessica has a really lovely ritual with her daughter. After bath-time they light a candle together in Ava's bedroom, as she gets her pyjamas on. They have a cuddle in bed and each talk about three things they are grateful for that day. Then, as Jessica leaves the room Ava blows out the candle and it's bedtime. Magic!

Action list:

- *Teach your Little Person to sleep unassisted*
- *Start with the 7pm bedtime and daytime naps using the settling techniques, and never take backwards steps*
- *Remember, it takes about two weeks of solid consistency to change behaviour, and only one slip-up to send you back to square one*
- *The key to these techniques is that you step closer and closer to the final goal of having your Little Person settle on their own. Don't get caught in a pattern of doing more and more. You will create a bigger problem long term*

NIGHT-TIME WAKE-UPS

There are three causes of night-time wake-ups:

1. The Little Person hasn't learnt to settle themselves and needs your help to get back to sleep.
2. Something has changed since they first went to sleep. The night light was on but now it's off, the music has ended, you were in bed with them but now you are gone, they had a dummy and it's fallen

out, they fell asleep on the boob/bottle and now it's gone, they fell asleep in your bed and woke up somewhere else, the list is endless.

3. They need something. Are they hungry, cold, in pain, thirsty, frightened or have a dirty nappy?

So what can you do?

TEACH THEM TO SELF-SETTLE

The first is to go back to the previous chapter and teach your child to go to sleep with as little help as possible. If you have to use sleep crutches at bedtime, make sure you can keep them consistent all night. Leave the light on or the CD on repeat. Teaching your baby to fall asleep by themselves usually takes 3-5 days.

DREAMFEED

For little babies that are waking hungry, sometimes a dreamfeed just before you go to bed can help get them through the night. A dreamfeed is where you gently pick up your baby, and feed them without waking them. Remember to gently burp your baby so that they don't wake up in pain or vomit.

MAKE SURE THEY ARE WARM ENOUGH

This is a big one. Many of the Little People I have worked with are cold at night and it wakes them up. If in doubt, add a layer or two. Remember, you probably have a nice warm partner keeping you warm and a big blanket. I often find Little People are put to bed in light cotton sleeping bags and get very cold.

Make the room really dark for really Little People. Babies like the dark. They are used to it from being in the womb and sleep better in the dark. Get some serious blackout blinds in the nursery. It will make a big difference to those babies that wake with the crack of dawn.

Older children who get frightened may need a dim night light. Especially once they need to take themselves to the toilet at night.

CHANGING NAPPIES IS WHAT YOU SIGNED UP FOR

If your Little Person poos at night there isn't much you can do. It's a stage and it won't last forever. The more they eat/drink during the night, the more they will poo.

'WAKE TO SLEEP'

Many sleep experts recommend using a technique called 'wake to sleep'.

This is when you have a *habitual waker* that will rouse at the same time every night. Often used for Little People that wake too early and need to learn to sleep-in to a reasonable hour.

The technique is to go into your Little Person and very gently rouse them 60 minutes before they would usually wake. (SO if they always wake at 5am, go in at 4am). Wake them just so they twitch, maybe their eyes will flutter. Don't fully wake them up. This resets their sleep cycle and often helps them sleep longer. Do this for 3–5 days in a row or until the habitual waking time changes. For naps they say to go in *30 minutes after they fall asleep*. It takes a bit of trial and error to learn how much waking and what is the best time to do it is, but I have seen this technique make a big difference. The main downside is that you have to set an alarm and wake up anyway, but if it buys you a few more hours in the long run, sometimes it's worth it!

The mattress by the bed

If your Little Person has nightmares, gets frightened during the night or is used to sleeping in your bed and now you are changing the rules, try this.

Have a small mattress or a piece of foam in your room that the child can sleep on. They will feel secure because they are near you, but they aren't in your bed. The best part about this one is it can become 'self-serve' comfort. Teach them to toddle in at 3am, drag their own pillow and doona and you might not even have to wake up! Got two children? Have a mattress on each side of your bed. This option doesn't seem to be as addictive as sleeping in bed with you.

Three in the morning isn't a good time to be making important decisions. Have a plan that is easy to follow before you start trying to change anything. Make it easy for yourself.

Action list:

- *Figure out what is causing night time wakeups*
- *Make a plan to overcome whatever is waking your Little Person*
- *Sometimes it will take a bit of experimentation and trial and error to figure out what the cause of the waking is. I promise, it won't last forever*

JACK-IN-THE-BOX BEDTIMES

Do you have a Little Person that thinks bedtime is a great time to play? Like a Jack-in-the-box, as soon as you have put them into bed (and sat down to finally enjoy some Big People time) they are back! Over and over again this happens until you feel like raging and they begin to fall apart because they are so overtired.

I see this all the time and the best approach for this one is attention removal with a massive dose of *follow through*.

Both the chair method and 'I'll be back in five minutes' techniques are great for these Little People. They will both backfire if you reward negative behaviour (like getting out of bed) with a positive consequence (any attention). This means no talking, no eye contact, no talking to your partner about what is happening while your Little Person is in earshot. You really have to try to behave like you've not even noticed they are up (other than physically putting them back in bed).

Here is that chair method:

The method for Jack-in-the-box-bedtimes:

1. Talk about what is going to happen at bedtime, throughout the day, so your Little Person is aware.
2. Follow your five-step bedtime routine.
3. After you have said goodnight, turned out the lights etc., either sit in your Little Person's bedroom or leave the room. If you choose to stay in the room, sit quietly and give them no attention. Don't

talk, no eye contact. Just relax. Meditate.

4. If your Little Person gets up, take them back to bed or lay them back down. The first time say, "It's time for bed now, show me how you can go to sleep". The second time say, "It's sleep time now" and after that say NOTHING. No eye contact. No attention for negative behaviour. The idea is to make it so boring, sleep is more fun.

5. Keep going until they stay in bed and go to sleep.

6. Be consistent and follow through.

7. Eventually you will be able to graduate to the "I'll be back in five minutes" model.

I'll be back in five minutes

This one is particularly useful for a Little Person who is getting up to check that you are still there, or to see what they are missing out on. It is covered in more detail in the chapter 'teaching to self-settle' but here is the quick step by step:

1. Talk about what is going to happen at bedtime, throughout the day, so your Little Person is aware.

2. Follow your five-step bedtime routine and say your final goodnight.

3. Say 'I'll be back in five minutes to see how you are going' (If you think it will take less than five minutes for your Little Person to get up, choose a smaller number).

4. Go and do something noisy that your Little Person won't find to interesting. The dishes is always a great option.

5. Go back in after five minutes (or however many minutes you said) and give them a kiss.

6. Repeat steps three to five until they are asleep!

Action list:

- *Pick a start date*
- *Don't start until all Big People are truly committed*
- *Remember that it will only get easier as long as you keep going*
- *Follow through!*

22. Tantrums

Around the age of 18 months, we delight in our Little Person's new ability to make demands, control their environment and generally wield their little wands about. That is, until they realise that they can use their newfound power against us.

Let's talk about those earth-shattering tantrums and how we can avoid as many as possible, and a few techniques for making them stop once they begin!

- Make sure your Little Person has all their basic needs met. Even the most angelic child can be monstrous when tired or hungry. If it's nearly nap time, skip the last minute trip to the supermarket if you can. And if you can't? Be prepared for a battle.
- Make a game of things you know your toddler isn't a fan of. If it's fun

and they are laughing, it's much easier to avoid the tears. Packing away can look very much like basketball. Shopping is definitely a treasure hunt. 'When we get to the supermarket I need three apples and a box of tissues. Think you can help me to find them?'

- Explain what you expect them to do in advance so they know how to please you. Trust me, they want to please you, and praise is the best reward for your Little Person. 'I'd like you to hold my hand all the way to the park gate please. Once we are inside, you can run around.'

- Avoid yes or no questions. 'Do you want to eat your broccoli?' will get a 'No!' every time. Try saying something like, 'It's time to eat your ...' or 'It's your turn now'.

- Distract them. You can feel a massive tantrum brewing. What's the best thing to do? Focus on something totally different. If you can, change the environment. Go outside. Spot a plane. 'What colour is that one? Do you think it's Qantas? Or Jetstar?' Before they know it, they will have forgotten all about that kid taking their ball.

- Blame someone else. Your Little Person doesn't think brushing their teeth is such a good idea. But they have to. You know why? Because the Dentist said so. This suddenly makes the brushing less optional (and you aren't the Bad Guy for once). Don't forget to make it a game as you move on!

- Always let them know what is coming next. Toddlers live in the moment. They are totally engrossed in whatever they are doing. When you just pull them away from their work without warning, they will often get disappointed and cross. Usually a 5-minute and a 1-minute heads-up will be enough. When starting this one, try to stick to the times. While Little People don't have a strong concept of time, it's important we give them consistent expectations of how long '1 minute' is.

- Make it sound worth it. If you ask your Little Person to come to you with a monster voice, do you really think they will come?

- Behave the way you expect your Little Person to behave. No screens at the table? Well put your own phone away. Monkey see, monkey do. It's not fair to expect them to do something you won't. This is also a great tip for eating. Eat with your toddler and show them how you can clean your plate!

- Ignore it! So you've had your 'last go' after giving a 1-minute warning but there is still a monster kicking and screaming on the floor. You said you had to leave, so make them believe it. Gather your things and off you trot. They will come running. You have to put on a convincing show though. (Once my car was right by the park gate, so when a Little Person kicked up a stink about leaving the park, I went and hopped in. She watched me, but wasn't convinced. So I turned on the car. She never tried to stay behind at the park again after that).

Now, it is important to know that there are two very different types of tantrums. There are the classic 'temper tantrums' which are the kind this chapter deals with, and there are true 'distress tantrums'. So what's the difference?

TEMPER TANTRUMS

- Are about control and manipulation
- Usually don't have real tears
- Are aiming to get something like food, a toy or attention
- Often happen as a result of digging-in heels ('you can't make me')
- Occasionally a temper tantrum can escalate into a distress tantrum

DISTRESS TANTRUMS

- Are when your child is literally out-of-control
- They are experiencing *big feelings* like rage, fear or separation anxiety
- They don't know how to manage their feelings
- They can't think or communicate properly
- They need help in the form of physical comfort and emotional empathy

Sometimes the best way to manage a very distressed child is to get behind them, grab their arms and cross them as if in the foetal position, squeeze them, speak reassuringly and wait

If your Little Person is a repeat offender with the good old temper tantrum, the next page has a list of all the reasons why this may be happening.

Because it's working.

Drama aside, if your Little Person is having tantrums regularly, it is an indication that they are using it as a tool to get what they want. It means that at some point they have thrown a massive wobbly and got the outcome they were hoping for. The quickest way to nip temper tantrums in the bud?

- Never let them work.
- Ignore these tantrums because they aren't nearly as appealing or rewarding without an audience.
- Follow through when you say No.
- Avoid trying to reason, argue or negotiate with a tantrumming child.
- Remain emotionally calm.
- It is okay for your toddler to have a tantrum. Don't try to stop it. That's not your job. *Just let it pass.*

Action list:

- *Learn to recognise a temper tantrum*
- *Make sure your Little Person has all their basic needs met*
- *Make boring things fun by turning it into a game*
- *Explain what you expect them to do in advance so they know how to please you*
- *Avoid yes or no questions. Make it an 'or'*
- *Distract them*
- *Always let them know what is coming next*
- *Behave the way you expect your Little Person to behave*
- *Ignore, ignore, ignore*

23. Mealtimes

Going to sleep and eating are the two main things your toddler is in complete control of. In a battle of the wills, they will win on these ones. We need to change the way the battle is geared, so that the eating (and sleeping) are a product of the battle – not the battle itself.

Somewhere between twelve and eighteen months your Little Person will decide that throwing food is great fun. They will also play a game where they drop things over the side of their highchair to see how many times you will pick it up for them. (Control lesson 101). They have also learned to screw up their face and turn away when they are full in order to signal, 'I don't want that'. Now, most parents are really pleased with their Little Person who will gobble anything they put in front of them. Until this stage starts. If your Little People are older, you may remember these stages. If you've picked up this book early enough, please take note that even the most well-intentioned Big People can accidentally fall into the 'chicken nuggets five nights a week' thing. Nobody does that on purpose. I'm going to show you how it happens.

The screwed up 'no thanks' face is where it all starts. This is great when you have a massive bowl of mush that you are steadily shovelling in, and your Little Person lets you know they are full. Then, your Little Person gets sick. Sick children will stop eating, even before you – or they – know they are sick. Again, this is a very useful tool we have developed. It means your Little Person's body can use all of its resources to fight the germs instead of digesting food. So your Little Person screws up their face. But you, as the Big Person, think, "Hmmm, you don't like carrot anymore. That is okay my precious bundle of joy. I will get you some yoghurt instead. You *looooove* yoghurt. And I couldn't put you to bed with no dinner". And your Little Person *does* love yoghurt. So even though their appetite is telling them not to eat, they do.

Now, a lesson that your Little Person has just learnt is that if they refuse what you first offer, they will get something else and that is something tastier. And you don't realise that, at the ripe old age of 13 months, your Little Person is manipulating you to get what they want.

What happens next? Little People start refusing things all over the place. Things that they used to love. Things they would eat with no problems only yesterday. And now, they won't touch it. So we, as loving Big People, add to the list of things we no longer offer. There are all sorts of valid reasons why we gradually narrow down our menu. It's a waste of food when they don't eat it. We don't want to have a fight at the end of the day. If they don't eat enough, they will wake up at two o'clock in the morning and they will be starving.

The problem with not offering the foods that kids "don't like" is that a child will not eat anything that seems unfamiliar to them. That means that at least the first three times that they see a little Broccoli tree on their plate. *They will not touch it.* I assume this is another primal instinct designed to keep us from poisoning ourselves. So, eventually, if you don't catch this early enough, you end up with a pre-schooler that eats a small selection of white things. In my experience this is usually pasta, white bread, cheese, the occasional piece of fruit, cereal with no milk (but lots of milk from a bottle), plus anything that comes in a packet that is really high in sugar. Think yoghurt, crackers, chips, lollies, biscuits etc. Oh, and

How to Be the Big Person Your Little Person Needs

if you're lucky, maybe raw carrot, beans or cucumber.

So what can you do to avoid this fate?

Keep food interesting and varied. As soon as you start making baby food, be creative. I've found babies love random things like mushroom, capsicum and squash purée. I make little frozen cubes of all sorts of fruits, veggies, meats and grains. Then mix and match to keep the little ones interested. Little People are learning about the world using their five senses. Food is a huge part of this. Different tastes and textures, slippery spaghetti and crunchy crackers. It's fascinating stuff – just like swishing jelly through your teeth and smooshing pear through your fingers.

As they grow, they get preferences for certain foods, which is great. They will begin to refuse food. That doesn't necessarily mean they don't like it. It could be because they aren't hungry or they are bored of that particular food. They might be unwell or just not 'feeling' the colour red that particular day. If you keep offering them just the things you know they like and will eat, beware. Kids, like adults, get bored of eating the same foods and will quickly start refusing the stuff they once loved.

It's important to remember that Little People generally won't eat something they don't recall seeing before. That means that you should expect to offer those olives at least three times before they will be interested in tasting them. So don't give up. Make a point of putting little decorations on the plate over and over again, just so your Little Person can get familiar with new things. If, after five appearances there hasn't been a nibble, encourage them to have a taste.

If your Little Person point blank refuses to eat what you offer without tasting it, tell them that it's fine that they aren't hungry and excuse them from the table. If they *aren't hungry enough for dinner, they aren't hungry enough for something else.* When they ask for food, continue to offer them their dinner. *Don't make them something else.* This is a trap I see so often. Parents prepare three meals every night, toddler eats none and takes the final option (usually dessert or a bottle before bed).

They are quick to catch on, whichever path you choose. And remember a child will *never* starve themselves.

A quick note on bottles

- Nearly every family I have helped to overcome food battles have had Little People that are still having bottles. Kids aren't hungry if they are full of milk *and* they know to save space for it after dinner.
- It is widely recommended that babies are weaned off the bottle at 12 months.
- Too much cow's milk can cause an imbalance in two ways: firstly, it is high in energy (calories); and secondly, it contains a lot of calcium.
- Too much calcium can cause iron deficiency, which has been linked to fussy eating.
- The RDI for calcium in toddlers is 500mg. Let's look at how much calcium is in your Little Person's diet:
  o Two cups of milk (500ml) = 590mg calcium, just exceeding the RDI
  o 30g of Cheddar cheese = 255mg
  o 200g of plain yoghurt = 342mg
  o 50g of tinned salmon = 155mg
  o Half a cup of baked beans has 40mg of calcium
- Calculate how much calcium your Little Person is getting. Is it more than one cup of milk and a bit of cheese? It is very easy to exceed the 500mg recommended intake of calcium in Little People!
- The other problem with milk is how many calories it contains. Toddlers need between 1200 and 1500 calories a day. If a two-year-old drinks just 300ml of milk, they've consumed 20% of all of their calories for that day – from just one food source. Then because they are feeling full they will begin to refuse other foods, and possibly become deficient in other nutrients.
- The sugars in milk make it very damaging for teeth to drink bottles in bed.
- Lying flat with a bottle can cause ear infections, always prop up your Little Person.

[Women and children's health network, nutrition department. Nutrition Australia]

Action list:

- *Don't offer something else*
- *Watch out for snacks*
- *Let them be hungry*
- *Don't argue over food, just let it go. Don't make their problem become your problem*
- *Ditch the bottles ASAP after their first birthday. Before they get really attached to the idea*

24. Sibling Rivalry

Arguments between brothers and sisters are totally normal and to be expected. Sibling rivalry is one of the ways that Little People learn the importance of respecting other people's feelings and belongings. It is also one of the ways children learn to sort out problems.

Learning to argue fairly and without hurting each other at home will help children to learn how to sort out issues in their other relationships in the future.

Remember, the child who *seems* to start the arguments is not always the one who does so. Often, one Little Person will do something to annoy the other one, knowing they will react and then get into trouble.

Here are some ways you can help to have fewer arguments in your house:

- Role model. How do you and your partner argue? How do you talk to each other? How do you talk to the Little People? Monkey see, monkey do.
- Ignore fighting as much as you can. When it gets heavy or too annoying, remind them that if they can't play nicely together, they can play separately in different rooms. Then follow through. This gets pretty boring pretty fast, so usually it will end the squabble.
- Defend the needs of each Little Person. For example, prevent older children's work from being wrecked by younger children and vice versa.
- Spend special time with each child on a regular basis. One-on-one time just before bed is a good ritual to have.
- Let each Little Person choose a few things that they can keep for themselves and not share. When they squabble over sharing, remind them that they have their own special toys.
- Make 'calling time-out' a thing in your house. We all need space, and it's great to have a system where you and your Little People can call time-out and take some much needed space every now and then.
- Try to keep things fair, but explain that your children are very different, so you love them in different ways.
- 'When you are his age, you can do that too' always works.
- One cuts, one chooses! This is where you get one child to cut a food treat in equal portions, and then their siblings choose which one they want. (You have never seen more equal portions).

Action list:

- *Role model. Monkey see monkey do. How would you like your Little People to behave?*
- *Ignore fighting as much as you can*
- *When it gets heavy or too annoying, remind them that if they can't play nicely together, they can play separately in different rooms*
- *Spend quality time with each child on a regular basis*
- *Explain that if ever someone Big or Little, is feeling overwhelmed they can 'call time out' and spend some time alone*

25. CHORES

If you want to keep children's feet on the
ground, put some responsibility on their shoulders

• a meme I saw once

Giving Little People chores is a great way to keep them busy, learning and useful. After all what is the point of having minions if you don't put them to work?

You can get your Little People helping out around the house from a very young age and increase their workload as they grow up. Little People love to feel valued and helpful and getting them to do chores is a great way to give them some responsibility. Really Little People begin as a helper. They watch and learn and will eventually graduate to doing these tasks on their own. This list is a guideline only. You know your Little People and what they are capable of and also what needs to be done around your house. Remember to praise them as they learn new skills, even if they don't do things as well as you can. Seeing how much they are 'helping' you will make them want to do more.

Here are some ideas for you:

Chores for Little People aged two and three

- Put toys away
- Put dirty clothes in laundry
- Feed pets
- Pass washing or the pegs, up to be hung out
- Wipe up spills
- Help unstack dishwasher
- Take plates to the kitchen
- Put their rubbish in the bin
- Help carry the recycling out
- Help to fold clothes
- Dust
- Pack away craft things
- Help to put clothes away

Chores for Little People aged four and five

All of the above, plus:
- Make their bed
- Unpack school bag and lunchbox
- Bring in the mail
- Put washing in and out of the washing machine (Front loader and remember to clear the area of toxic chemicals first).
- Set the table
- Help to sweep
- Pick up after pets
- Water the garden
- Unload utensils and plastic from dishwasher
- Wash plastic dishes at the sink

- Fix a bowl of cereal
- Pair up socks

Chores for Little People aged six and seven

All of the above, plus:
- Sort the laundry
- Take the rubbish and recycling out
- Bring the empty bins back in from the street
- Put clothes away
- Sweep floors
- Set and clear the table
- Unstack the dishwasher
- Help to pack away shopping
- Wipe down tables and benchtops
- Help to make and pack lunches
- Weed and rake leaves
- Keep the bedroom tidy
- Chop with a butter knife

Chores for Little People aged eight and over

All of the above, plus:
- Put away the shopping
- Vacuum
- Help to make the dinner
- Tidy up after themselves
- Wash the table after meals
- Put away own laundry
- Make own breakfast
- Clean the kitchen
- Peel vegetables
- Change their bed sheets
- Cook simple foods, such as toast
- Mop the floor
- Tidy and sort their things
- Make their own snacks

- Clean pet cages
- Take pet for a walk
- Load and unload the dishwasher
- Fold the laundry
- Clean the bathroom
- Wash the windows
- Wash the car
- Cook simple meals with supervision
- Iron clothes
- Do the laundry
- Supervise younger siblings (with Big People in the home)

Action list:

- *Find some things to delegate around your house*
- *Teach your Little Person how to do those jobs*
- *Perhaps start a chart to help them keep on track*

26. Aggression

Violence is something that can be disciplined without giving a warning. Children need to know that hitting, kicking, biting, etc. will never be tolerated.

FOR YOUNG BABIES AND FIRST TIME OFFENDERS

When they hurt you

When training a puppy not to bite, as soon as the little guy sinks its teeth into you, you need to react instantly. A quick, loud response is recommended by dog trainers, (often accompanied by a jab with the fingers to simulate the nip a mother dog would give). While I am not suggesting you simulate biting your child, I do recommend the loud 'Ouch', pulling away quickly, turning your back and dramatically nursing whichever part they hurt. This uses very loud non-verbal communication to tell your child in their language that they have hurt you and they shouldn't do that again. No lecture required.

When they hurt others

Remove them from the situation, give them a firm reprimand. This could be the universal 'Ah-ah' for babies or a longer, 'Oh dear, poor Benny! No kicking. Kicking hurts' for an older child. It is important then to tell the Little Person what you do want. So after giving them a minute to process, take them back to the hurt child say, 'Sorry' together and say, 'We need to be gentle with our friends, show me how you can be gentle'. Demonstrate a gentle stroke on the other child's arm, and get your Little Person to do the same. Finish up with, 'That's better. Gentle.' Then watch your child like a hawk, and be ready to do the whole process again. If your Little Person is taking some time to learn about inflicting pain, try to avoid strangers' children.

FOR OLDER CHILDREN

When they hurt you

React in the same way as you would with a baby, but spend some more time talking to your Little Person about what they did, and how it made you feel. Also offer a blanket warning: 'If you ever do that again then I will <insert discipline>' and of course, follow through.

When they hurt others

Again, the message is the same as it would be with a baby, but now you can use more words and less actions. After your quick response discipline ask them how they would feel if someone did that to them. Ask them what they could do differently next time.

For repeat offenders

Learn what triggers your child's violent response and try to predict it coming. When you see them getting wound up, talk to them about how they are feeling and what they could do about it, without hurting anyone. You could say something like, 'I know you are feeling frustrated that your brother is drawing on your work, maybe you could call some time-out and take your colouring into your room'.

Action list:

- Get clear on where the boundaries are around aggressive behavior
- Have a conversation with your Little People and make sure they are clear on these boundaries in a calm moment
- Have a plan for consistent discipline ready and follow through when necessary

THANK YOU

Congratulations on reading this book! I know it's not an easy feat with Little People around. I'd like to take this opportunity to say *thank you* for reading it. I hope that you have learnt some new strategies and ideas that you have put into action. If you haven't started acting yet *do it now!*

Your Little People are great teachers and some of the greatest lessons in life you will learn from them. Revel in the gift of being able to see things through a child's eyes for the second time around. Don't be afraid to take time to look after yourself (remember babysitters are significantly cheaper than psychologists!). Use the ABCs in this book to create an extraordinary foundation for your relationship with your children and don't forget to have *fun!*

I'd like to leave you with one last quote from my mother, who really is the best mother one could hope for.

> "When you were young, I considered myself as a bank balance - if all I did was make withdrawals, I would soon be bankrupt. It was essential to make deposits for my own well-being".

See. Even the *best* needs time out.

ABOUT CLAIRE

In the last ten years, Claire has been lucky to work with hundreds of children and their families. Some for a very short term and some for over eight years! In this time, Claire has gained huge insight into what makes kids tick as well as what makes them flip.

Claire is on a mission to help parents and toddlers get along brilliantly so everyone feels calm, happy and well-rested. She is inspired to do this because she has often seen the flipside – where family life is chaotic and everyone feels frustrated and exhausted – and knows from experience it doesn't have to be this way.

Claire has noticed that practically every family will have battles over things like eating, sleeping or other behaviour.

To help families to overcome these problems, Claire developed Angelic Monsters, a program that sets up positive patterns of behaviour for kids that last well into their teenage years.

Claire helps families to see how simple strategies can create stronger bonds and happier Little People who thrive. Ideally, she works with toddlers and pre-schoolers from 18 months to 7 years of age.

Claire transforms Little People's behaviour by working with entire families in their homes. She teaches tried-and-tested techniques that work to END food, sleep and control battles for good so that families can enjoy outstanding relationships with their Little People.

She does this because she knows that even the most challenging 'terrible-two-year-old' can be an absolute angel, depending on how the Big People around them behave, respond and communicate.

Claire has encouraged absolute transformations in both Big and Little People. Many start out as strung out and not coping – then become harmonious families, who really enjoy spending time together and creating beautiful memories every day.

To submit your *success stories* for a second edition of this book, ask a question or give feedback, please email claire@angelicmonsters.com

If you are interested in further help to be the Big Person your Little Person needs, through engaging Claire to speak, joining a program or engaging Claire to create a tailored package for you, then please visit www. angelicmonsters.com.au/contact or email claire@angelicmonsters.com.